HISTORIC LOS ANGELES ROADSIDES

BY MIMI SLAWOFF

REEDY PRESS

DEDICATION

To my family: Bruce, Christina, Michael, and Megan
And in memory of my parents, Stoitcho and Slatka Slawoff

Reedy Press
PO Box 5131
St. Louis, MO 63139
reedypress.com

Book Design: Julie Sturma

All photos by Mimi Slawoff unless otherwise noted.

Library of Congress Control Number: 2024949383

ISBN: 9781681065793

25 26 27 28 29   5 4 3 2 1

CONTENTS

Manhattan Beach residential street

INTRODUCTION

Historic Los Angeles Roadsides blends history, travel, and photography that showcase LA's network of scenic, classic roadways that wind through 80 diverse towns.

These roadways, often just two lanes, travel through beach towns, mountains, valleys, deserts, and urban streets. Along the roadways, themselves an interesting part of the journey, are many opportunities to pull over and enjoy vistas, historic sites, unique attractions, and locally owned establishments.

Some of these roadways are relatively short, others longer. And several can be combined via gateway cities. For example, historic Route 66 ends in Santa Monica, where you can hop on Pacific Coast Highway (PCH) in time to catch a beach sunset.

Even as a native Angeleno, I continue to discover new places. Road trips are exciting! I love eating at old-school diners on Route 66, perusing whimsical boutiques in Topanga Canyon, and touring historic beach homes along PCH.

Historic Los Angeles Roadsides includes listings for locally owned restaurants and hotels (mostly no chains), as well as fun things to do.

While each section features a town's history from California statehood, it's important to acknowledge that the land was first inhabited by Indigenous Peoples, including the Cahuilla, Tonga, Shoshone, and Chumash. The arrival of Spanish and American settlers gradually developed Southern California.

Mission bells placed along streets and highways throughout California mark what is believed to be the original route of El Camino Real, linking California 's 21 missions.

ACKNOWLEDGMENTS

Scott Piotrowski (president, California Historic Route 66 Association), Crescenta Valley historian and author Mike Lawler, Joanna Linkchorst, Maria Wessenhauer, and my friend Donna Shiroma, who joined me on most road trips.

DESTINATIONS AND DETOURS

These pages include communities that are not directly on a historic roadway but are nearby. No matter which roadways you choose, enjoy the ride.

Palmdale
Pearland
Four Points
Alpine
Pearblossom
Ritter Ranch Park
Agua Dulce
Vincent
Acton
Crystalaire
Canyon County
ANGELES NATIONAL FOREST
SAN GABRIEL MTS.
Hidden Springs
San Dimas
ANGELES NATIONAL FOREST
Sheep Mountain Wilderness
San Gabriel Wilderness
San Gabriel Reservoir
Sylmar
San Fernando
Pacoima
Hansen L.
Sunland-Tujunga
FERNANDO VALLEY
La Crescenta
Burbank
Montrose
La Cañada Flintridge
Altadena
Glendale
North Hollywood
Sierra Madre
Pasadena
Monrovia
Azusa
Glendora
San Dimas
Duarte
Encino
Sherman Oaks
Studio City
Universal City
Glassell Park
Eagle Rock
South Pasadena
San Marino
Arcadia
Claremont
Hollywood
Highland Park
Garvanza
Irwindale
La Verne
Los Angeles
West Hollywood
E. Hollywood
Mt. Washington
Silver Lake
Cypress Park
El Sereno
Montclair
Beverly Hills
Echo Park
Lincoln Heights
Downtown Los Angeles
South El Monte
Pomona
Century City
Santa Monica
W. Los Angeles
Chinatown
Walnut
Diamond Bar
Little Tokyo
E. Los Angeles
View Park
Windsor Hills
Huntington Park
Hacienda Heights
Venice
Marina del Rey
Ladera Hts.
Inglewood
Pico Rivera
Rowland Heights
Chino
Whittier
La Habra Hts.
Cudahy
Santa Fe Springs
La Habra
Chino Hills
Playa del Rey
Lennox
Athens
Lynwood
S. Whittier
Brea
El Segundo
Lawndale
Paramount
La Mirada
Buena Park
Fullerton
Yorba Linda
Manhattan Beach
Placentia
Hermosa Beach
Artesia
Cerritos
La Palma
Redondo Beach
Torrance
Carson
Anaheim
Villa Park
Palos Verdes Estates
Lomita
Signal Hill
Los Alamitos
Stanton
Wilmington
Rossmoor
Garden Grove
Long Beach
Rancho Palos Verdes
Westminster
Midway City
Seal Beach
E. Tustin
Tustin
Santa Ana
San Pedro
Fountain Valley
San Pedro Bay
Sunset Beach
Huntington Beach
Costa Mesa
Lake Forest
Irvine
Newport Beach
Laguna Woods
Laguna Hills
Aliso Viejo
Laguna Beach
Laguna Niguel

ROUTE 66

Famous Route 66 was established in 1926 as the nation's first federal highway. Simultaneously, the introduction of the automobile made it possible for people to take road trips across eight states. Around the same time, Hollywood made its debut as a world film capital. Since then, people have been making the drive from the start of Route 66 in Chicago to Los Angeles. The entire route spans over 2,440 miles.

As driving and road trips became popular, the Automobile Club of Southern California was instrumental in developing the popularity of Route 66 by providing signage and maps with directions to Southern California—where the historic highway spans 315 miles.

In Los Angeles, Route 66 travels about 75 miles through 31 towns from Claremont to Santa Monica, where it ends at Olympic and Lincoln Boulevards.

Over time, Route 66's popularity created overcrowding on the highway, resulting in the construction of new interstates that eventually replaced portions of US 66.

In Los Angeles, Route 66 was realigned several times, often changing names in various cities. Route 66 in the San Gabriel Valley became Foothill Boulevard and Huntington Drive. Traveling west, Route 66 became Santa Monica Boulevard through Hollywood and Beverly Hills to Santa Monica.

There were five different Route 66 paths between Old Town Pasadena and Downtown Los Angeles. This book follows the 1932–34 Transitional Alignment for directions that best represent Route 66 in the Lower Arroyo Seco and Northeast Los Angeles communities. Historic Route 66 signs are posted along many streets.

TO START THE TOUR, BEGIN AT FOOTHILL AND INDIAN BOULEVARDS IN CLAREMONT and drive through 31 cities and neighborhoods as you zigzag through LA and end at the Route 66 sign at Lincoln and Olympic Boulevards in Santa Monica.

Claremont Heritage, housed in the historic Garner House, serves to preserve the town's historic places.

CLAREMONT

Claremont is a pretty university town anchored by the Claremont Colleges (which comprise seven private colleges).

The town was established with citrus ranches and the Santa Fe Railroad in 1887. Claremont was incorporated in 1907.

Claremont was among 30 town sites developed in anticipation of a population boom resulting from the arrival of the railroad. However, that didn't happen, and many of the other town sites became railroad ghost towns. What saved Claremont was the transfer of the Hotel Claremont and 260 vacant lots by the local land company to the newly founded Pomona College in 1888. The college is among the consortium of the Claremont Colleges.

Thanks to Frank Wheeler (known as the father of Foothill Boulevard), Foothill Boulevard became part of Route 66 in Claremont in 1931. Wheeler and Ralph Cornell designed the layout for eucalyptus trees to line the highway, establishing Claremont as the City of Trees.

After WWII, the citrus industry diminished as land was sold off for the housing boom in the 1950s. By the early 1970s, the industry was finished.

Historic places include the Spanish Colonial Revival Garner House, built by Herman and Bess Garner in 1926. The City of Claremont purchased the house and its surrounding citrus groves in 1946 to create Memorial Park. In 2001, Claremont Heritage moved to the home.

Original buildings from Route 66 are located along Foothill Boulevard and include Wolfe's Kitchen & Deli (founded in 1917) and the boat-shaped Tugboat Annie's restaurant (currently vacant).

Visit!

CLAREMONT HERITAGE
840 N Indian Hill Blvd.
909-621-0848

CLAREMONT CITY HALL
207 Harvard Ave.
909-399-5460

SUMNER HOUSE
An 1887 Queen Victorian house.
105 N College Ave.

RUTH CHANDLER WILLIAMSON GALLERY AT SCRIPPS COLLEGE
251 E 11th St.
909-607-2029

TUGBOAT ANNIE'S RESTAURANT
A historic but currently vacant structure.
962 W Foothill Blvd.

CLAREMONT UNITED CHURCH OF CHRIST (1891)
233 Harrison Ave.
909-626-1201

Eat!

CLAREMONT VILLAGE GRILLE (1920)
148 N Yale Ave.
909-626-8813

SOME CRUST BAKERY (1889)
119 N Yale Ave.
909-621-9772

THE BACK ABBEY
128 N Oberlin Ave.
909-625-2642

VIVA MADRID
225 N Yale Ave.
909-624-5500

WOLFE'S KITCHEN & DELI (1917)
160 W Foothill Blvd.
909-626-8505

to Do!

CALIFORNIA BOTANIC GARDEN
Established in 1927, the garden features California's native plants and habitats.
1500 N College Ave.
909-625-8767

CLAREMONT DEPOT
Built in 1887 and replaced in 1927 in the Spanish Colonial style; houses the Claremont Lewis Museum of Art.
200 W 1st St.
909-621-3200

CLAREMONT FARMERS & ARTISANS MARKET
(8 a.m. to 1 p.m., Sundays)
Harvard Ave. at Second St.

CLAREMONT PACKING HOUSE
Historic building from 1916 to 1945 and now housing various establishments.
532 W First St.
909-623-0535

Stay!

CLAREMONT LODGE
736 S Indian Hill Blvd.
909-626-5654

HOTEL CASA 425
425 W 1st St.
909-624-2272

TIP

Step back in time on a self-guided walk in Claremont Village, home to historic structures and locally owned shops and restaurants.

claremontheritage.org
discoverclaremont.com

The Claremont Depot houses the Claremont Lewis Museum of Art.

TO REACH POMONA, continue west on Foothill Boulevard.

POMONA

Located within the Pomona Valley is the City of Pomona, which incorporated in 1888. With a population of about 146,000, Pomona is a large city with economically diverse neighborhoods representing generations of residents.

The Don Ygnacio Palomares and Don Ricardo Vejar families were among the first settlers. Today's Adobe de Palomares Museum sits on the site where Ygnacio and Concepción Palomares built a 13-room house from 1850 to 1854. It was abandoned in the 1880s and acquired by the City of Pomona in the 1930s.

The arrival of the railroad in the 1870s expanded Pomona's agricultural industry, inspiring horticulturist Solomon Gates to name Pomona after the Roman goddess of fruit.

Meanwhile, Louis Phillips, a Jewish immigrant from Prussia, started a new town called Spadra and built his mansion there in 1875. Spadra flourished for a while with three stores, a school, and a post office. But it was eventually

The one-story Adobe de Palomares is one of Pomona's oldest structures.

Phillips Mansion

annexed by Pomona, and today only the Phillips Mansion and Spadra Cemetery still exist. The Pomona Historical Society bought the Phillips mansion for $45,000 in 1966 and maintains the house and cemetery.

Pomona's most recognized attraction is Fairplex, the grounds for the Los Angeles County Fair, which debuted in 1922. When attendance dipped during the Great Depression, the Federal Works Progress Administration helped boost the local economy by employing workers to construct permanent exhibition halls and other buildings. During WWII, the Fairplex grounds were used as a temporary camp for Japanese Americans. Currently, Fairplex hosts various events and has an on-site train museum and art center.

TIP

The Pomona Historical Society offers monthly tours of Spadra Cemetery; the nearby Phillips Mansion; and the 1907 Currier House, the former residence of sheriff, state senator, and philanthropist A. T. Currier.

pomonahistorical.org

Eat!

MAMAS PUPUSAS
1038 E Holt Ave.
909-743-0048

POMONA VALLEY MINING COMPANY
1777 Gillette Rd.
909-623-3515

ROOKERY ALEHOUSE AND GRILL
171 W Second St.
909-865-4400

XPHO VINA
281 S Thomas St.
909-865-6777

to Do!

THE POMONA FAIRPLEX
Home to the RailGiants Train Museum, a farm, and many events, including the Los Angeles County Fair.
1101 W McKinley Ave.
909-623-3111

Visit!

ADOBE DE PALOMARES MUSEUM
491 E Arrow Hwy.
909-623-2198

PHILLIPS MANSION
2640 Pomona Blvd.
909-623-2198

CONTINUE WEST ON FOOTHILL BOULEVARD
into and through La Verne.

LA VERNE

Founded in 1887 by Los Angeles businessman Isaac Wilson Lord, the town was originally called Lordsburg. He successfully convinced the Santa Fe Railroad to extend its line through the town where he owned property, and he invited people for a free ride to his new town. Hundreds of people bought lots, and the town gained water mains, a post office, stores, and a newspaper.

The area attracted members of the Church of the Brethren, who formed a congregation and started a college in the vacant Lordsburg Hotel in 1891—today the respected University of La Verne.

Other settlers were ranchers who planted field crops and citrus trees. The first ranching family was L. H. Bixby's. Residents voted to rename the city La Verne in 1917, after the death of Lord (who had opposed a name change in 1912).

By 1919, the city was producing and shipping thousands of carloads of oranges, lemons, and grapefruit. During this period, nearly everyone in the community was involved in the citrus industry.

La Paloma is located on Route 66.

Large Craftsman houses were built in the 1920s, but new construction ended with the Great Depression. Citrus sales and college enrollment dropped. During WWII, thousands of people came to California for military service or to work in war industries. Citrus groves were sold for housing developments.

Present-day La Verne is a mix of residential, commercial, and industrial areas.

La Paloma, located along Route 66 on Foothill Boulevard, has been serving Mexican food for over 49 years. It was called Wilson's in the early days.

Eat!

LA PALOMA MEXICAN RESTAURANT
2975 Foothill Blvd.
909-593-7209

MI COCINA MEXICAN GRILL
2232 D St. #101
909-929-0780

to Do!

THE BRIDGE TO NOWHERE TRAIL leads to the 120-foot arch bridge that spans the East Fork of the San Gabriel River. The five-mile (each way) trail crosses a stream. The trailhead is on Camp la Bonita Rd. Weekdays are less crowded.

CONTINUE WEST ON FOOTHILL BOULEVARD into and through San Dimas.

SAN DIMAS

San Dimas is known for Raging Waters Los Angeles, a popular water park built in 1983. But in the 1800s the community was known for another kind of water, the swampy Mud Springs marsh. Mud Springs was the community's first name.

After the arrival of the Santa Fe Railroad in 1887, the San Jose Land Company laid out streets and lots, and E. M. Marshall opened the first business—a hardware store. Mud Springs was renamed San Dimas.

The San Dimas Hotel was built in 1887 in anticipation of a land boom that never happened. Two years later, the property was sold for $25,000 to James W. and Sue Walker. Still standing, it's known as the Walker House and is home to the historical society and a restaurant.

Prior to incorporating in 1960, San Dimas had numerous citrus groves, four citrus packing houses, and a marmalade factory. The agricultural industry faded as San Dimas developed in the mid-1900s. The city's oldest business, the San Dimas Feed Company, opened in 1897 and still exists as San Dimas Grain Co., a pet store.

San Dimas embraces its heritage with a Western-style downtown. And the Pacific Railroad Museum, housed in the historic Santa Fe Railroad Depot, contains signal equipment, model trains, and railroad publications.

The original depot, which opened in 1889, was destroyed by fire in 1933. It was replaced the following year with the current Art Deco–style building and operated until 1961.

Nearby, the Martin House was built by William Malcolm Martin in 1901 and serves as home base for the San Dimas Chamber of Commerce.

The San Dimas Hotel (a.k.a., the Walker House) is on the National Register of Historic Places.

Eat!

INHOUSE COFFEE
942 W Arrow Hwy.
909-447-0782

TWISTED SAGE CAFÉ & CATERING
433 E Foothill Blvd.
909-305-0724

SWEET SAVORY CAFÉ & BAKERY
138 W Bonita Ave. (Frontier Village Shopping Center)
909-305-9738

ROADY'S RESTAURANT
160 W Bonita Ave.
909-592-0980

VINCENZO'S TERRAZZA AT WALKER HOUSE
(a.k.a., the San Dimas Hotel)
121 N San Dimas Ave.
909-394-3311

Visit!

PIONEER PARK
225 S Cataract Ave.
909-394-6200

SAN DIMAS HOTEL
(a.k.a., Walker House)
121 N San Dimas Ave.

MARTIN HOUSE
246 E Bonita Ave.
909-592-3818

PACIFIC RAILROAD MUSEUM
210 W Bonita Ave.
909-394-0616

to Do!

RAGING WATERS LOS ANGELES
111 Raging Waters Dr.
909-802-2200

SAN DIMAS CANYON NATURE CENTER
Hiking trails and picnic areas.
1628 Sycamore Canyon Rd.
909-599-7512

TIP

Stroll through the historic Western-themed downtown. Relax in Pioneer Park, which has picnic tables and a basketball court.

225 S Cataract Ave.

The San Dimas Feed Company is the city's oldest business and now operates as the San Dimas Grain Co.

AS YOU ENTER GLENDORA, Foothill Boulevard becomes Route 66. You have two options: The Historic Alignment (1926–1932) goes north on Amelia Avenue, then west on Foothill Boulevard, rejoining the Bypass Alignment at Foothill and Alosta Avenue in front of the Azusa Foothill Drive-In Theatre.

The Bypass Alignment continues west on Route 66, which becomes Alosta Avenue in Azusa, and rejoins the Historic Alignment at Azusa Foothill Drive-In Theatre.

GLENDORA

Artifacts from the Shoshone have been found in the Glendora area, which opened for homesteading in 1868. The first American settlers were John Bender and William Bryant Cullen, childhood friends from Memphis, Tennessee. They homesteaded land and planted wheat, barley, flax, grapevines, vegetables, and fruit trees. During the 1870s, more farmers arrived.

In 1885, George D. Whitcomb left Chicago for Southern California and purchased 200 acres for $40 per acre. He named the city Glendora from "Glen," describing the narrow valley on his property, combined with part of his wife Leadora's name.

Glendora was officially founded in 1887 and incorporated in 1911 with 700 residents. In the next decade, churches and schools were built, and streets were graded and named. Whitcomb named east–west streets for family members and north–south streets after states or places he lived. Foothill Boulevard was originally called Minnehaha Avenue.

The city grew rapidly during the 1950s and 1960s. The completion of the Foothill Freeway through Glendora in 1973 connected the city with other Southern California cities.

Rubel Castle was built by Michael Clarke Rubel and hundreds of volunteers from 1968 to 1986. The whimsical castle is made from local river rock and salvaged materials.

The Glendora Historical Society, housed in the first city hall building from 1913, maintains the Glendora Museum and Rubel Castle, a folk architecture structure—both are located north of the Foothill Boulevard alignment of Route 66 in town.

Glendora is the first community in LA County in which Route 66 had multiple alignments, with the original alignment following Amelia Avenue north to Foothill Boulevard before continuing west. The more current alignment maintains a straight path onto present-day Route 66, formerly Alosta Avenue.

A historic roadside stop on Route 66 includes the Frank Chance Building (known as the Cub Building), built in 1912 by Chicago Cubs first baseman Frank Chance.

Eat!

ED'S PLACE
141 N Glendora Ave.
626-335-6630

FRISELLA'S ROASTERY
179 N Glendora Ave.
626-852-1810

KARA'S KORNER
101 W Foothill Blvd.
626-914-7447

LUCA BELLA FINE FOODS
216 N Glendora Ave.
626-963-5500

RAMON'S TACOS Y TAPAS
146 N Glendora Ave.
626-852-2111

STACKS ON ROUTE 66
640 W Route 66
626-852-9444

STUBBORN MULE GLENDORA
180 N Glendora Ave.
626-335-0034

SUSHI NI
201 N Glendora Ave.
626-335-9911

THE DIPLOMAT JUNIOR
171 N Glendora Ave.
626-335-7795

VILLAGE EATERY
221 N Glendora Ave.
626-852-1777

TIP

Enjoy a meal at Stacks, a diner that is decked out in Route 66 decor. Known for its pancakes, the diner also makes good sandwiches (try the patty melt). Stay the night in the historic Route 66 Palm Tropics Motel, still in its original cottage-style design with landscaped gardens.

Stay!

PALM TROPICS MOTEL
619 W Route 66
626-914-4702

to Do!

Schedule a tour at **RUBEL CASTLE**, built by Michael Rubel and his friends over several years. They completed it in 1986.
844 N Live Oak Ave.
626-963-0419

ROUTE 66 CONTINUES THROUGH AZUSA on Foothill Boulevard.

AZUSA

Wednesday, May 20, 1868: "The school house was finished. Beckman and others prepared the stools, desks, etc., and prepared to hire a teacher."

This excerpt from the diary of Henry Dalton, a wealthy Englishman who acquired land in Azusa in 1844, describes the steps taken to provide the area's first school for the community.

However, the first documented reference to Azusa is found in the diary of Father Juan Crespi, an engineer with the Portolá Expedition in 1769. He wrote about the tall mountain range, stream, and valley, and he referred to the area as the Azusa. The name was possibly derived from the Shoshone tribe, whose community was known as Asuksa-nga. However, some historians say the name comes from the saying "everything from A to Z in the USA."

Like its neighbors, the city developed from an agricultural and citrus region into a residential and industrial area. When Azusa was subdivided in

The reference to Henry Dalton's diary is found on the Azusa Historical Society's website at azusaca.gov/569/Azusa-History

1887, some people paid as much as $500 for first-choice lots.

As Azusa's population grew, schools were built. The first public school was built of logs and brush. To see an example of a colonial Craftsman-style home, visit the Durrell House, built by Azusa mayor M. T. Durrell in 1923. For a nostalgic glimpse of Route 66, drive by the marque from the Azusa Foothill Drive-In Theatre, which showed movies for 40 years until 2001. The final showings were *Harry Potter and the Sorcerer's Stone* and *Ocean's Eleven*. At night, the marquee is lit up in neon pink and incandescent white bulbs.

TIP

Put on your walking shoes and explore Azusa's beautiful canyons and forests.

Eat!

CONGREGATION BREWERY & COCINA
619 N Azusa Ave.
626-334-2337

DOG HAUS BIERGARTEN AZUSA
638 N Azusa Ave.
626-633-9090

LA TOLTECA
429 N Azusa Ave.
626-334-0302

Visit!

AZUSA FOOTHILL DRIVE-IN THEATRE
675 E Foothill Blvd.

to Do!

DURRELL HOUSE MUSEUM
The original location was on Route 66.
740 N Alameda Ave.
626-334-1382

CONTINUE WEST THROUGH IRWINDALE on Foothill Boulevard.

IRWINDALE

Irwindale is a small but thriving community (population about 1,413) that evolved from a mining community to a manufacturing and high-tech city in the heart of the San Gabriel Valley.

The community was first settled by the Gregorio Fraijo and Fecundo Ayon families in the 1850s. Each generation stayed in the area, and today there are seven generations of native Irwindale residents descended from the two families. Irwindale was incorporated in 1957.

Irwindale, which has a prosperous sand and gravel industry, has over 700 businesses and serves as headquarters for several major national companies, including Ready Pac, Irwindale Brew Yard, and Charter Communications.

The Irwindale Speedway opened in 1999 for short track racing and as a gathering spot for car enthusiasts. It was renamed Irwindale Speedway & Event Center in 2013 and was home to NASCAR races, demolition derbies, festivals, and street-legal racing. When there was talk of demolishing the venue, former Irwindale Late Model racer and track champion Tim Huddleston took over management in 2018 to keep it open. However, the venue was scheduled to permanently close in December 2024.

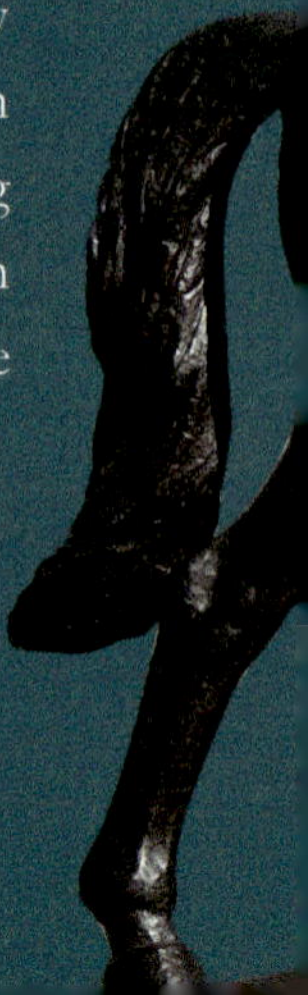

AS YOU ENTER DUARTE, Foothill Boulevard becomes Huntington Drive. Continue west through Duarte on Huntington Drive.

DUARTE

Located across the street from City Hall, a bronze statue of Andres Avelino Duarte pays homage to the city's founder. Duarte, who was born in Mission San Juan Capistrano in 1805, joined the Mexican army and was assigned to Mission San Gabriel in his early 30s.

In 1841, ex-corporal Duarte was granted 7,000 acres of land in the upper San Gabriel Valley by the governor of Alta California. Naming the land Rancho Azusa de Duarte, he planted crops and ranched the property. In the mid-1850s, he sold most of the ranch to pay off debt.

Dr. Nehemiah Beardslee purchased some land, started the first school, and laid out the first section of water lines. As pioneer families settled in Duarte, it became a thriving agricultural community specializing in citrus production. When Duarte was incorporated as a city in 1957, it evolved from an agricultural area to a suburban community. Several cities were established on land originally granted to Duarte. These include the neighboring towns of Monrovia, Azusa, Irwindale, Baldwin Park, Arcadia, and Bradbury.

TIP

Visit the Duarte Historical Society & Museum, which has exhibits about Route 66 and artifacts that celebrate the city's history. Free admission

777 Encanto Pkwy., 626-357-9419

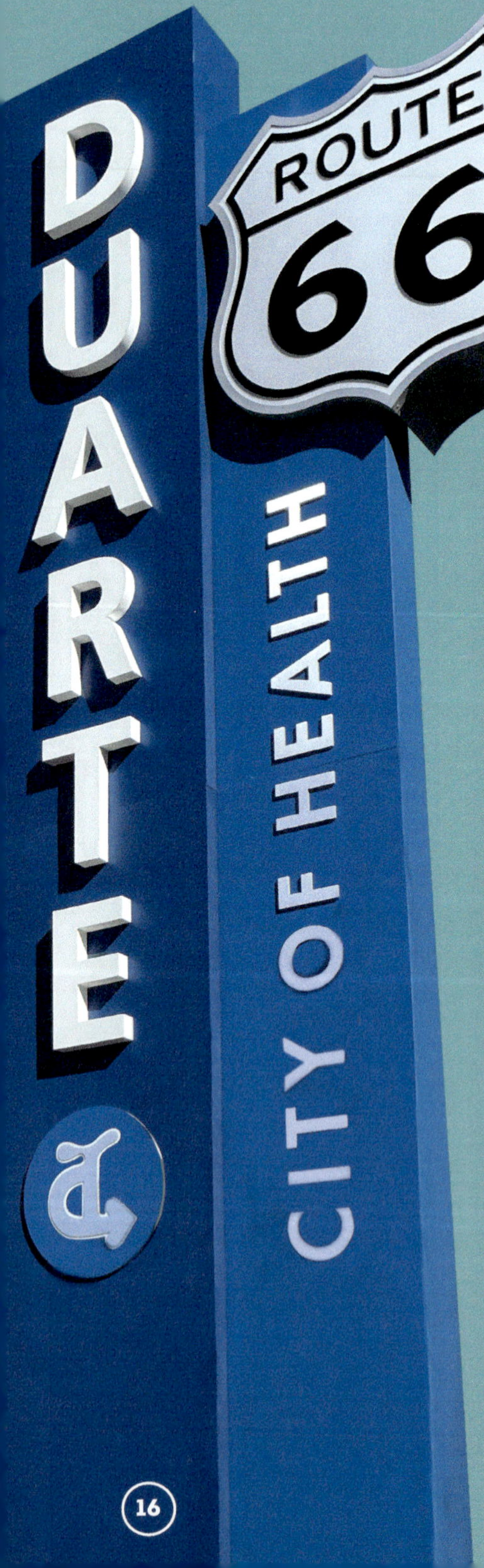

Eat!

ROUTE 66 ROADHOUSE & TAVERN
1846 Huntington Dr.
626-357-4210

Visit!

ANDRES AVELINO DUARTE STATUE
1584 Calle Andres

CONTINUE WEST ON HUNTINGTON DRIVE to Monrovia. You have two options here: The Historic Alignment turns north on Shamrock (there's a former filling station at Shamrock and Walnut), then west on Foothill Boulevard. This historic route continues west on Foothill through Arcadia into Pasadena. It veers south on Sierra Madre Boulevard, then west on Colorado Boulevard, joining the Bypass Alignment.

The Bypass Alignment continues through Duarte and Arcadia on Huntington Drive. At Santa Anita Park it veers northwest onto Colorado Place, then west onto Colorado Boulevard. At Sierra Madre Boulevard, it rejoins with the Historic Alignment.

Former filling station built in the Spanish Mission style at Walnut and Shamrock Avenues.

MONROVIA

Monrovia is a quiet but social little town with weekly street fairs and farmers markets. It was platted in 1884 when William N. Monroe purchased land, formed the Monrovia Land and Water Company, and sold lots around present-day Colorado Boulevard and Myrtle Avenue—the main thoroughfare through town and home to mom-and-pop businesses.

To prevent an unwanted saloon from moving in, Monrovia incorporated on December 15, 1887, and passed a "tippler's" law, prohibiting the sale of alcohol.

Monroe built a home, known as the Oaks, for his family at 250 North Primrose that still stands today. He and his family are buried in Live Oak Cemetery on Duarte Road.

Pacific Electric Railway arrived in Monrovia in 1903, bringing more growth to the city.

Historical sites include the defunct 1927 Flying A Gasoline Station built in the Spanish Mission style at Walnut and Shamrock Avenues. It's one of only two Flying A stations left in Los Angeles County. The filling station has been used in several movies to replicate roadside stations of the 1920s to 1940s.

Built in 1925, the Aztec Hotel is Monrovia's most popular landmark. It was designed by architect Robert Stacy-Judd in the Mayan Revival architectural style and has been listed on the National Register of Historic Places since 1977. Although the Aztec Hotel closed to guests in 2011, the on-site Mayan Bar & Grill is open.

Eat!

ALITALIA PIZZERIA
899 W Foothill Blvd.
626-359-7235

BASIN 141 SOCIAL BAR & KITCHEN
402 S Myrtle Ave.
626-249-0358

CAFÉ DE OLLA
423 S Myrtle Ave.
626-238-6300

GREY & CASH
425 S Myrtle Ave.
626-239-2220

JAKE'S ROADHOUSE
622 S Myrtle Ave.
626-599-9453

LORD EMPANADA
1540 S Myrtle Ave.
626-415-1044

SUNDAY'S OLD TOWN BISTRO
520 S Myrtle Ave.
626-303-7100

THE MONROVIAN
534 S Myrtle Ave.
626-359-8364

THE PEACH CAFÉ
141 E Colorado Blvd.
626-599-9092

Stay!

OAK PARK MOTEL
925 E Huntington Dr. (Route 66)
626-358-1148

Visit!

MONROVIA HISTORICAL MUSEUM
742 E Lemon Ave.
626-357-9537

to Do!

FRIDAY MONROVIA STREET FAIR & MARKET
(5 p.m. to 10 p.m.)
700 S Myrtle Ave.
626-256-8246

SATURDAY MONROVIA FARMERS MARKET
(9 a.m. to 2 p.m.) Station Square Park
1629 S Myrtle Ave.
626-256-8246

TIP

The Monrovia Historical Museum occupies a building that once housed the municipal swimming pool. Known as "The Plunge," it operated from 1925 to 1983. The former dressing rooms now comprise the museum's two exhibit wings, including the Historic Monrovia Wing, which highlights the Monroe family's role in establishing the city.

CONTINUE WEST on Foothill Boulevard through Arcadia.

Visit!

GILB MUSEUM OF ARCADIA HERITAGE
380 W Huntington Dr.
626-574-5440

ARCADIA

Some people have a knack for good luck. That seems to be true of Elias Jackson "Lucky" Baldwin, who purchased the Rancho Santa Anita land grant and subdivided the area in the 1870s. Baldwin, Arcadia's first mayor, earned the nickname "Lucky" for his good fortune in business investments.

Arcadia was incorporated on August 5, 1903. With a climate conducive for agricultural purposes, poultry raising became the largest business. Many large poultry farms supplied eggs and meat to Los Angeles markets. Soon city streets were graded and paved, and streetlights were installed, creating an urban community.

Baldwin's passion for horse racing led to the development of the Santa Anita Park thoroughbred racetrack in 1907. It closed in 1909, burned in 1912, and reopened on Christmas Day in 1934.

The plaque commemorating racehorse jockey George M. Woolf and Seabiscuit is along the Thoroughbred Walk of Champions on Huntington Drive.

The Derby was called the Proctor Tavern when it was founded by Hudson M. Proctor in 1922.

TIP

Explore themed gardens and historic structures at the 127-acre Los Angeles County Arboretum and Botanic Garden. The Queen Anne Cottage was built by Elias Jackson Baldwin in 1885–86.

arboretum.org

Los Angeles County Arboretum & Botanic Garden

Toward the end of World War I, the Ross Field US Army Balloon School was established, bringing in thousands of servicemen. The site is now Arcadia Park.

Throughout the years, the horse-racing community has influenced the city. In 1922, the Derby restaurant opened near the racetrack as a gathering spot for jockeys and race fans. The Thoroughbred Walk of Champions features bronze plaques with names of horses, jockeys, trainers, and owners along Huntington Drive.

In 1947, California and the City of LA established the Los Angeles County Arboretum and Botanic Garden here, showcasing themed gardens and historic structures.

Stay!

LE MÉRIDIEN PASADENA ARCADIA
130 W Huntington Dr.
626-777-6699

Eat!

THE DERBY
233 E Huntington Dr.
626-447-2430

MT. LOWE BREWING CO.
150 E St. Joseph St.
626-244-7593

to Do!

LOS ANGELES COUNTY ARBORETUM & BOTANIC GARDEN
301 N Baldwin Ave.
626-821-3222

SANTA ANITA PARK
(thoroughbred racetrack)
285 W Huntington Dr.
626-574-7223

TAKE COLORADO BOULEVARD through Pasadena and into Old Town.

PASADENA

Pasadena has many outstanding attractions, but its crowning glory is the annual Tournament of Roses Parade and Rose Bowl game on New Year's Day.

The parade's history began on January 1, 1890, four years after the city was incorporated. To showcase the city's sunny climate, the Pasadena Valley Hunt Club launched a winter festival with horses and carriages decked out in flowers.

The parade was formally sponsored by the Tournament of Roses Association in 1898. Since then, the 5.5-mile parade takes place each year with floral floats, marching bands, equestrian units, and public officials. In 1961, the rose was adopted as Pasadena's official flower.

The Rose Bowl, which follows the parade and is home to the UCLA Bruins football team, was built in 1922 in the Arroyo Seco. The venue is used for various events, including a large swap meet.

The 23-square-mile Pasadena is a walkable city with over 30 historic and landmark districts. You'll see many landmarks in Old Pasadena, also called

View of historic Colorado Street Bridge from Desiderio Neighborhood Park.

Old Town. The 22-block area has quaint alleyways, 200 specialty shops, bistros, and entertainment venues. Public art is displayed throughout.

Pasadena is also known for its 19th-century architecture. The Pasadena Civic Center anchors the Beaux Arts Mediterranean Revival–style Pasadena City Hall (1927), Pasadena Central Library (1927), and the Pasadena Civic Auditorium (1932).

The Gamble House, an architectural example from the American Arts & Crafts movement, was built in 1908 for David and Mary Gamble of Proctor & Gamble. The exterior appeared as Doc Brown's house in *Back to the Future.*

Other historic sites include the 150-foot-high Colorado Street Bridge, completed in 1913.

The Norton Simon Museum's Sculpture Garden surrounds a pond decorated with water lilies.

to Do!

The **BOBA TRAIL** features 30-plus boba shops along Route 66. Boba is a Taiwanese tea beverage with milk and tapioca balls.

GAMBLE HOUSE
4 Westmoreland Pl.
626-793-3334

PASADENA PLAYHOUSE
39 S El Molino Ave.
626-356-7529

ICE HOUSE COMEDY CLUB (1960)
24 N Mentor Ave.
626-414-2386

Eat!

ARROYO CHOP HOUSE
536 S Arroyo Pkwy.
626-577-7463

LA GRANDE ORANGE & LUGGAGE ROOM PIZZERIA
Located in the historic 1934 Del Mar Train Station.
260 S Raymond Ave.

MIJARES MEXICAN RESTAURANT (1920)
145 Palmetto Dr.
626-792-2763

THE RAYMOND
Established by Walter Raymond in 1886, the Raymond was a grand hotel until it burned to the ground in 1895. Although it was rebuilt, it was razed in 1931 to make way for residential development. The caretaker's cottage is now the Raymond restaurant.
1250 S Fair Oaks Ave.
626-441-3136

TIP

Stroll through Old Town to shop, eat, and admire public art. While in Old Town, look for "ghost signs"—lettering from old signs hand-painted on brick walls that have chipped and faded over the years.

Visit!

CANTERBURY RECORDS
805 E Colorado Blvd.
626-792-7184

CASTLE GREEN
Built in 1898 as an upscale resort. Later, it was divided into 50 individually owned units, and is an event location.
99 S Raymond Ave.
626-793-0359

EATON CANYON NATURAL AREA
1750 N Altadena Dr.

PASADENA CITY HALL
100 N Garfield Ave.
626-744-7507

PASADENA MUSEUM OF HISTORY
470 W Walnut St.
626-577-1660

PASADENA VISITORS CENTER
300 E Green St.
626-795-9311

ROSE BOWL STADIUM
1001 Rose Bowl Dr.
626-577-3100

USC PACIFIC ASIA MUSEUM
Dedicated to the arts and culture of Asia and the Pacific Islands.
46 N Los Robles Ave.
626-787-2781

VROMAN'S BOOKSTORE
695 E Colorado Blvd.
626-449-5320

TOURNAMENT HOUSE AND WRIGLEY MANSION
Headquarters for the Tournament of Roses and Rose Bowl Game. (Tours are available at 2 p.m. Thursdays April through August. Reservations required)
391 S Orange Grove Blvd.
626-449-4100

NORTON SIMON MUSEUM
411 W Colorado Blvd.
626-449-6840

Stay!

PASADENA HOTEL & POOL (1926)
928 E Colorado Blvd.
626-884-4150

HEAD SOUTH out of Old Town Pasadena on Fair Oaks to South Pasadena. Proceed west on Mission Street. Go left onto Pasadena Avenue and veer right to continue onto Pasadena Avenue.

SOUTH PASADENA

Unless you live here, it would be easy to confuse South Pasadena with Pasadena when you're looking for a specific address. For example, Fair Oaks Boulevard, which follows Route 66, travels seamlessly through both cities. But addresses differ. The two cities are distinct in many ways, starting with size.

Just 3.44 square miles, South Pasadena is a compact, tree-lined city with family-owned businesses along Fair Oaks Avenue and Mission Street, and historic homes nestled among apartments in tidy residential neighborhoods. It's a walkable city with hometown family events. Incorporated on March 2, 1888, South Pasadena was one of the first suburbs of Los Angeles.

The establishment of the Raymond Hotel in 1886 and the Cawston Ostrich Farm in 1896 attracted tourists and new residents to the area. Although these two no longer exist, South Pasadena has preserved several historic structures.

The Rialto Theatre opened for vaudeville and movies on October 17, 1925, and featured a Wurlitzer pipe organ. The theater changed ownership a few times and showed its final movie in 2007. It was added to the National Register of Historic Places in 1978. In 2017, the Mosaic church on Hollywood Boulevard signed a 15-year lease with the theater.

Fair Oaks Pharmacy & Soda Fountain on Route 66

Bissell House

The historic Bissell House, built in 1887, was home to Anna Bissell McCay, a Pasadena philanthropist and daughter of vacuum magnate Melville Bissell. The elegant Victorian-style house is now a bed and breakfast (and historical landmark) situated on a quiet corner.

TIP

The South Pasadena Farmers Market offers fresh California produce and prepared food from 4 p.m. to 8 p.m. every Thursday.

920 Meridian Ave.
626-403-2820

Eat!

BISTRO DE LA GARE
921 Meridian Ave.
626-799-8828

CANOE HOUSE
805 Fair Oaks Ave.
626-799-4169

COMMUNAL FOOD AND DRINK
1009 El Centro St.
626-345-5128 (call for reservation for parties of six or more)

COS & PI
303 Pasadena Ave.
626-460-6030

FAIR OAKS PHARMACY & SODA FOUNTAIN (1915)
1526 Mission St.
626-799-1414

FIORE MARKET CAFÉ
1000 Fremont Ave.
626-441-2280

GUS'S BBQ
808 Fair Oaks Ave.
626-799-3251

HI-LIFE BURGERS
1326 Fair Oaks Ave.
626-799-5401

MAMMA'S BRICK OVEN
1007 Fair Oaks Ave.
626-799-1344

NICOLE'S MARKET & CAFÉ
921 Meridian Ave., Unit B
626-403-5751

SHAKERS
601 Fair Oaks Ave.
626-799-9168

THE MUNCH COMPANY
1028 Mission St.
626-441-1036

Visit!

GARFIELD PARK
1000 Park Ave.
626-403-7200

SUGARMYNT GALLERY
810 Meridian Ave.
626-222-7257

WAVERLY BOOKSTORE & CAFÉ
1010 ½ Fair Oaks Ave.
626-460-6027

Stay!

BISSELL HOUSE
201 Orange Grove Ave.
626-441-3535

THE ARROYO VISTA INN
335 Monterey Rd.
323-478-7300

to Do!

FREMONT CENTRE THEATRE
Performing arts theater.
1000 Fremont Ave.
626-441-5977

GO LEFT ONTO PASADENA AVENUE, and then right to continue on Pasadena Avenue, which becomes York Avenue into Garvanza.

OR TAKE A THREE-MILE DETOUR TO SAN MARINO to visit the world-renowned Huntington Library, Art Museum, and Botanical Gardens. From South Pasadena, head south on Fair Oaks to Mission Street (left), to Garfield, (right) to Monterey Road (left), to Oxford Road (left). The Huntington has two entrance gates: Allen Avenue and Oxford Road.

DETOUR

SAN MARINO

San Marino is a small, affluent city (population about 12,000) that is home to the world-renowned Huntington Library, Art Museum, and Botanical Gardens, which opened to the public in 1928.

But its history dates to 1903, when railroad magnate Henry E. Huntington purchased a working ranch from landowner James De Barth Shorb, who together with Benjamin D. Wilson and George S. Patton played key roles in developing San Marino.

In 1854, Benjamin Davis Wilson established his Lake Vineyard Ranch home on Euston Road. As Mayor of Los Angeles and a state senator for two successive terms, Wilson entertained prominent Southland visitors to his home. When his daughter, Maria, married James De Barth Shorb, he gifted them an adjoining property, where they built their San Marino Ranch.

The Shorbs hosted many guests, including Huntington, who later (after James De Barth Shorb's death) purchased the property and built a mansion to house his collection of books and paintings. He hired William Hertrich to develop the gardens, starting with lily ponds.

The lily ponds were the first area developed at the Huntington

The Huntington Art Gallery is housed in the Huntington's former residence.

The Huntington Art Gallery depicts the Huntington's lifestyle.

Huntington's, Wilson's, and Patton's primary ranchos, along with subdivided areas and smaller ranchos, were incorporated as the city of San Marino in 1913—the same year that Huntington married Arabella.

While the Huntingtons lived in the mansion, they amassed extensive library, art and botanical collections. In 1919, they signed a trust document to establish their estate as a public collections–based, research and educational institution. It opened to the public in 1928.

The Huntington features a library containing more than 12 million items, an art museum with over 45,000 objects, and 16 themed gardens spanning 130 acres.

Visit!

EDWIN HUBBLE HOUSE
A historic house and private residence in San Marino. Built in 1925, it was the home of astronomer Edwin Hubble.
1340 Woodstock Rd.

EL MOLINO VIEJO
(also known as the Old Mill)
1120 Old Mill Rd.
626-449-5458

LACY PARK
1485 Virginia Rd.
626-300-0790

SAN MARINO HISTORICAL SOCIETY
The Thurnher House is open to the public on the first and third Sundays of every month from noon to 3 p.m.
1475 Virginia Rd.
626-304-9375

to Do!

Explore **THE HUNTINGTON LIBRARY, ART MUSEUM, AND BOTANICAL GARDENS** on your own, or take a tour. The first Thursday of every month is free of charge with advance reservation. Free day tickets are available the last Thursday of every month. 10 a.m. to 5 p.m. (closed Tuesdays)
1151 Oxford Rd.
626-405-2100
huntington.org

GARVANZA

An ad in the *Los Angeles Times* in 1886 promised health benefits and land for homes and farms to those who moved to Garvanza. At the time it was in the very early stages of development. In 1869, Andrew Glassell and Alfred Beck Chapman bought the land and sold it to businessmen and brothers Ralph and Edwards Rogers. The land was named Garvanza for the garbanzo bean fields in this area.

The Rogers brothers, who were real estate developers, subdivided the land and sold lots. The area experienced a real estate boom in the late 1800s and early 1900s, becoming a popular neighborhood with Victorian and Craftsman-style homes. Artists, writers, musicians, and other creative people moved in, attracted by the town's natural setting, proximity to LA, and inexpensive properties.

Garvanza was annexed in 1899 by the City of Los Angeles and is a district in Highland Park. In the 1940s, the construction of the Arroyo Seco Parkway connected Los Angeles and Pasadena, making Garvanza more accessible and contributing to its growth.

Judson Studios

The family-owned Judson Studios, a stained glass company since 1897, has its headquarters in Garvanza. In 2016, Judson Studios opened a fused and kiln-formed glass studio in nearby South Pasadena.

to Do! On a two-hour **JUDSON STUDIOS PUBLIC TOUR** learn about the company's history and how it designs and fabricates its stained glass, fused glass, and architectural glass. Registration is required.
judsonstudios.com
200 S Ave. 66, 323-255-0131

TURN LEFT (SOUTH) ON FIGUEROA STREET to enter Highland Park. Continue on Figueroa through Highland Park.

HIGHLAND PARK

Highland Park was once an independent city before being annexed to the City of Los Angeles in 1895, making it one of LA's first suburbs. Open space offered respite to city dwellers. Soon, the establishment of art communities and colleges transformed the rustic community into a hub for intellectuals and artists.

The main street, Figueroa Street, was part of the Transitional (1932–34) and Alternate (1936–40) Alignments of Route 66. This main drag was replaced on December 30, 1940, with the Arroyo Seco Parkway, which became Route 66. This made Highland Park the first community along Route 66 to be bypassed by a freeway. In Highland Park, Route 66 is Figueroa Street, a main street with numerous restaurants, businesses, and historic structures, including Fire Station No. 12, operating since 1903.

Since the 1920s, Highland Park has attracted artists and much of their work can be seen around town. In Highland Park Bowl, there's a forest

The 1933 Group acquired the 1927 bowling in 2014 and restored the bowling lanes, ball-return machinery, bow-truss ceiling, and other features.

mural painted above the lanes by the Anderson Brothers in the 1930s during the Arts and Crafts movement.

Highland Park is still known for street art featuring murals and sidewalk mosaics along Figueroa Street and York Boulevard.

Unique landmarks include Chicken Boy, a 22-foot-tall fiberglass statue (half human and half poultry) that was formerly signage for a chicken restaurant. Now it stands atop a restaurant on Figueroa Street.

Two historic signs along Figueroa have been relit through community efforts: the Highland Theatre rooftop sign (5604 North Figueroa) and Manning's Coffee Store sign (5705 North Figueroa).

to Do!

Go bowling at **HIGHLAND PARK BOWL**, which opened in 1927 during Prohibition. The US Treasury Department authorized physicians to write prescriptions for medicinal whiskey, enabling the venue to serve drinks to bowlers. After the bowling alley fell into disrepair, the 1933 Group bought and restored the venue, complete with refurbished Brunswick pin machines sourced from 1949.
5621 N Figueroa St., 323-257-2695

Visit!

CHICKEN BOY STATUE
5558 N Figueroa St.

Eat!

AMIGA AMORE
5668 York Blvd.
323-739-0894

BAGEL + SLICE
4751 York Blvd.
323-739-9600

EL HUARACHE AZTECA
5225 York Blvd.
323-478-9572

GOLDBURGER
5623 York Blvd.
323-274-4303

HIPPO
5916 ½ Figueroa St.
323-545-3536

JOY
5100 York Blvd.
323-999-7642

LAS CAZUELAS RESTAURANT
5707 N Figueroa St.
323-255-4719

MACIEL'S PLANT-BASED BUTCHER SHOP
5933 York Blvd.
213-537-5120

PENNY'S BURGERS
6300 N Figueroa St.
323-254-7223

TACO JOE'S MEXICAN RESTAURANT
26659 Highland Ave.
909-864-4466

THE GREYHOUND BAR AND GRILL
5570 N Figueroa St.
323-900-0300

FROM HIGHLAND PARK, stay on Figueroa Street to Mount Washington, or as you approach Mount Washington, veer left onto Pasadena Avenue to enter Cypress Park.

The Charles Lummis House is a rustic American Craftsman stone house.

MOUNT WASHINGTON

(ROUTE 66 ALIGNMENT, 1932–34 AND 1936–40)

Mount Washington is a historic neighborhood in the San Rafael Hills of northeast Los Angeles. Developed in 1909 by Robert Marsh, Mount Washington was home to the Southwest Museum of the American Indian (LA's first museum) until 2022, when the museum's collections were moved to the Autry Museum in Griffith Park. The museum was founded by Charles Lummis, who built his American Craftsman–style home from stones in the late 19th and early 20th centuries.

Over the years, Mount Washington became a hub for artists and writers who were attracted to the area's hilly, winding streets. Mount Washington's cultural diversity is reflected in architectural styles that include Craftsman, mid-century modern, and contemporary.

The hilly neighborhood has winding, vertical streets, most notably Eldred Street, the steepest street in California. Built in 1912 before current city regulations, Eldred Street has a 33 percent grade. It's a residential area, but you can park at the bottom and hike about 400 feet to the top, where it dead ends at the wooden Eldred Street Stairs (about 195).

Visit!

Charles Lummis House
Also called El Alisal. It's open to the public on weekends.
200 E Ave. 43
323-226-1620

TAKE PASADENA AVENUE
to Cypress Park.

Top of steep Eldred Street, which borders Highland Park and Mount Washington

Pedestrians and bicyclists can cross the Los Angeles River via the Taylor Yard Bridge, which connects Cypress Park and Elysian Valley.

CYPRESS PARK

Named after cypress trees that once lined the banks of the Los Angeles River, Cypress Park is located at the confluence of the Los Angeles River and the Arroyo Seco.

It was an agricultural area in the 18th and 19th centuries before becoming an industrial town. Entrepreneur J. Hartley Taylor, who had a grocery store and feed mill and raised animals, made a name for himself when he gave up part of his land to the Southern Pacific Railroad to build a freight switching and maintenance yard facility along the banks of the Los Angeles River in 1911.

Named the Taylor Yard, the railway station handled the bulk of LA's freight traffic, which traveled through Cypress Park from the 1920s until it closed in 1985, following a gradual decline in railroad jobs. Deindustrialization and the arrival of freeways shifted the population and local economy.

But Cypress Park got a boost when the City of LA bought the Taylor Yard property. It was dismantled, leaving an open area that wildlife began reinhabiting.

In 2022, the bright orange Taylor Yard Bridge opened, enabling pedestrians and bicyclists to cross the Los Angeles River from Cypress Park and Elysian Valley. The 400-foot-long steel bridge, designed for pedestrian and bike use, is accessible via the LA River Bike Path.

TIP

To see the Taylor Yard Bridge, park at Rio de Los Angeles State Park, 1900 North San Fernando Road, and walk about half a mile to the bridge.

The tidy neighborhood alongside the LA River has a range of historic housing styles, including American Revival cottages and Craftsman and Mediterranean Revival homes with front yard gardens.

Eat!

EL ATACOR #1
3520 N Figueroa St.
323-342-0180

KING TACO
1118 Cypress Ave.
323-223-2595

Visit!

LOS ANGELES RIVER CENTER AND GARDENS
570 W Ave. 26
323-221-9944

to Do!

RIO DE LOS ANGELES STATE PARK
1900 N San Fernando Rd.
323-276-3015

IN LINCOLN HEIGHTS, at the five-point intersection, veer slightly right to stay on Pasadena Avenue.

Learn about the history of the LA River at the Los Angeles River Center and Gardens.

LINCOLN HEIGHTS

One of Lincoln Heights's most striking features is Lincoln Park, a scenic urban space with a large lake, fountain, and park amenities that include a playground, picnic tables, and ball fields.

It's one of LA's first parks, created by the city in 1881 from land donated by John Strother Griffin. Originally called East Los Angeles Park, then Eastlake Park, the urban space was renamed Lincoln Park on May 19, 1917. The new name reflected the name change for Lincoln Heights, which was called East Los Angeles from 1873 to 1917.

Also located in the park is Plaza de la Raza, a cultural center offering performing and visual arts since 1970.

Another delightful landmark is nearby San Antonio Winery, the oldest operating business in Lincoln Heights. The family-owned-and-operated winery and restaurant was founded by Italian immigrant Santo Cambianica in 1917. At that time, Los Angeles was a prime grape-growing and winemaking region. In 1970, the family added Maddalena Restaurant. Named after the founding year of the wine company, the 1917 Wine Bar & Bistro offers outdoor dining and wine tasting.

TIP

Take a walk around the lake in Lincoln Park, home to ducks and geese. Trees provide shade for a relaxing rest stop.

Eat!

MADDALENA RESTAURANT IN SAN ANTONIO WINERY
737 Lamar St.
323-223-1401

Visit!

MADDALENA RESTAURANT IN SAN ANTONIO WINERY
737 Lamar St.
323-223-1401

to Do!

SAN ANTONIO WINERY / 1917 WINE BAR & BISTRO
737 Lamar St.
323-223-1401

CROSS THE LOS ANGELES RIVER on the Broadway Bridge (Buena Vista Viaduct) and enter Chinatown. At the southern edge of Chinatown, turn right (west) onto Cesar Chavez/Sunset Boulevard.

CHINATOWN

The area's first Chinese immigrants, who arrived in LA in 1852, were mostly male and worked as laundrymen, market gardeners, road builders, and ranchers.

Despite discrimination in the late 19th century, these Chinese pioneers successfully established LA's first Chinatown on Alameda and Macy (now Cesar Chavez Avenue) Streets in 1880. It eventually encompassed about 15 streets and alleys with 200 structures and was a thriving residential and commercial community until 1910.

However, within a few years, discriminatory laws and economic challenges caused the community to decline. After 30 years of decay, it was razed in the early 1930s to make way for Los Angeles Union Station, the city's main transit hub for trains and buses, which opened in 1939. Meanwhile, with

Chinatown Central Plaza

East Gate, a five-tier Golden Pagoda, marks the entrance to Central Plaza.

the help of Peter SooHoo, a Chinese American born and raised in Old Chinatown, and Y. C. Hong, a social activist and immigration lawyer, a New Chinatown was established about a mile away. The grand opening was celebrated on June 25, 1938.

The Twin Dragon Gateway Monument marks the south entrance to Chinatown on North Broadway. East Gate, also known as the Gate of Maternal Virtue, was installed in 1939 on behalf of Y. C. Hong to honor his mother. The pedestrian plaza is home to pagoda-style buildings with red lanterns, dim sum houses, bakeries, gift shops, and specialty markets. Just inside Central Plaza's East Gate is a statue of Dr. Sun Yat-sen, the first president of the Republic of China.

Chinatown is also home to the Taoist Thien Hau Temple and the Chinese American Museum, which are housed in the historic Garnier Building. The 1890 Garnier Building is the last surviving structure from the city's original Chinatown.

TIP

Park on the street or in a lot and walk along Broadway, which is lined with gift shops and eateries, to Central Plaza, 943 Broadway.

A festive time to visit is during the Annual Golden Dragon Parade, hosted by the Chinese Chamber of Commerce of Los Angeles in February.

Eat!

PHOENIX BAKERY (1938)
969 N Broadway
213-628-4642

WON KOK RESTAURANT
210 Alpine St.
213-613-0700

Visit!

CHINESE AMERICAN MUSEUM
425 N Los Angeles St.
213-485-8567

Stay!

HOTEL FIGUEROA
939 S Figueroa St.
213-627-8971

to Do!

Guided walking tours of Chinatown are offered by the **CHINESE HISTORICAL SOCIETY OF SOUTHERN CALIFORNIA**. To schedule a tour, call 323-352-8824 or email info@chssc.org.

PASS OVER CESAR E. CHAVEZ AVENUE and continue south on Broadway to the original western terminus at Broadway and 7th. Turn west on 7th. Turn north on Figueroa. Turn west on Sunset Boulevard to rejoin post-1936 Route 66.

DOWNTOWN LOS ANGELES

Route 66 passes through the heart of downtown Los Angeles, and El Pueblo de Los Angeles Historical Monument marks the spot where 44 settlers of Native American, African, and European heritage established a farming community in 1781.

Learn more about their story at the state historic park, where you'll find many of the city's first structures, including a fire house, hotel, theater, and plaza. It's a fun way to learn about LA's early history after it was incorporated

Olvera Street

in 1850 and developed into a metropolis of 88 cities with over 10 million residents.

Also located here is Olvera Street, which was part of Route 66's early alignment. The colorful Mexican marketplace has shops, eateries, and festivals.

Across the street is Los Angeles Union Station, a transit hub built in 1939 in the Mission Moderne style. The beautiful station features Art Deco chandeliers, inlaid marble floors, and hand-painted mission tiles.

There are several historic sites by Route 66's original western terminus at Broadway and 7th. The Broadway Theater District anchors several movie theatres, including the Palace Theatre, which opened in 1911 as the third home of the Orpheum vaudeville circuit in LA. Nearby, the five-story Bradbury Building is an architectural landmark with a light-filled Victorian court. Pershing Square has been a public park and event space since 1866. Established in 1917, the open-air Grand Central Market is packed with an array of food and spice stalls that reflect the city's ethnic diversity.

While in the area, take a ride on Angels Flight, a historic funicular that opened in 1901 and travels from California Plaza at the top to the lower station on Hill Street.

Eat!

COLE'S
LA's oldest public house. Located in the historic Pacific Electric Building
118 E 6th St.

EL CHOLO
(Mexican restaurant)
1037 S Flower St.
213-746-7750

GRAND CENTRAL MARKET
317 S Broadway
213-359-6007

PHILIPPE THE ORIGINAL
1001 N Alameda St.
213-628-3781

Stay!

THE BILTMORE LOS ANGELES (1923)
506 S Grand Ave.
213-624-1011

TIP

Explore the historic district, ride Angels Flight Railway, and savor a meal in Grand Central Market. Choose from empanadas, tacos, chow mein, smoked meats, lobster rolls, pupusas, burgers, and more.

Visit!

BRADBURY BUILDING
304 S Broadway

EL PUEBLO DE LOS ANGELES HISTORICAL MONUMENT (AND OLVERA STREET)
125 Paseo de La Plaza
213-485-6855

LOS ANGELES CENTRAL LIBRARY
650 W 5th St.
213-228-7000

LOS ANGELES UNION STATION
800 N Alameda St.
213-452-0200

LOS ANGELES FLOWER MARKET
Wall St. between 7th and 8th Sts.

PERSHING SQUARE
532 S Olive St.
213-847-4970

THE LAST BOOKSTORE
453 S Spring St. (ground floor of the Spring Arts Tower)
213-488-0599

to Do!

ANGELS FLIGHT RAILWAY
350 S Grand Ave. (Top Station)
351 S Hill St. (Lower Entrance)

THE MUSIC CENTER
(see a show or take a tour of the campus)
Composed of the historic Ahmanson Theatre, Dorothy Chandler Pavilion, Mark Taper Forum, Roy & Edna Disney CalArts Theatre, and Walt Disney Concert Hall.
135 N Grand Ave.
213-972-7211

For area information, check out Discover Los Angeles, discoverlosangeles.com.

CONTINUE WEST ON SUNSET BOULEVARD through Echo Park.

DETOUR

LITTLE TOKYO

Little Tokyo is a walkable neighborhood a short distance from Union Station in Downtown LA. It's the second-oldest neighborhood in Los Angeles and was declared a National Historic Landmark in 1995.

Little Tokyo was first settled when Japanese seaman Hamanosuke "Charles Hama" Shigeta opened the Kame Restaurant on East First Street in 1885. In the late 1800s, many Japanese immigrants, mostly male, arrived to work as laborers in local agriculture. They stayed in boarding houses around East First Street.

By 1900, several more businesses had opened, establishing the first-generation Japanese American community with businesses, schools, and cultural institutions to meet the needs of the growing Japanese population.

During WWII, following the attack on Pearl Harbor, many Japanese were sent to internment camps, forcing the closing of their businesses. After the war, many returned to Little Tokyo to start fresh. Some were able to buy back their shops. The community once again experienced growth as new businesses opened.

The museum features historical and arts exhibitions about the Japanese American experience. Courtesy of Donna Shiroma

The family-owned Fugetsu-Do confectionery opened in 1903 and specializes in Japanese treats and mochi.

In the latter half of the 20th century, Little Tokyo experienced a cultural renaissance with festivals, art galleries, and local organizations committed to preserving Japanese heritage.

Eat!

DAIKOKUYA
327 E 1st St.
213-626-1680

FUGETSU-DO
315 1st St.
213-625-8595

KURA REVOLVING SUSHI BAR
333 E 2nd St.
213-290-9631

Visit!

JAMES IRVINE JAPANESE GARDEN
(in the Japanese American Cultural & Community Center)
244 San Pedro St.
213-628-2725

KOYASAN BUDDHIST TEMPLE
342 1st St.
213-624-1267

LOS ANGELES HOMPA HONGWANJI BUDDHIST TEMPLE
815 1st St.
213-680-9130

Stay!

ROYAL PAGODA MOTEL
(in Chinatown Central Plaza)
995 N Broadway
323-223-3381

to Do!

JAPANESE AMERICAN NATIONAL MUSEUM
100 N Central Ave.
213-625-0414

TIP

Visit the Little Tokyo Koban and Visitor's Center for maps and tips.

307 1st St., 213-613-1911

ECHO PARK

While constructing a new lake and park (to replace a reservoir) in 1892, architect Joseph Henry Tomlinson heard workers' voices from across the basin and realized the lake had a natural echo and coined the name Echo Park.

The area now known as Echo Park was called Edendale until about the 1940s and was home to film studios before Hollywood took the spotlight.

William Selig built the first permanent movie studio at Clifford Street and Glendale Boulevard. Mack Sennett founded Keystone Studios and introduced slapstick comedy. The Keystone Cops films (about bumbling cops) often filmed in Echo Park. The studio was mostly torn down, but there's a commemorative plaque at 1712 Glendale Boulevard.

Echo Park developed into a residential community in the late 19th and early 20th centuries and was known as a bohemian and artsy area. By the 1950s, the entertainment industry had moved out of Edendale and into major Hollywood studios.

Echo Park Lake has swan-shaped pedal boats and walking paths.

When Dodger Stadium, home to the Los Angeles Dodgers of Major League Baseball, was built in the Chavez Ravine in 1962, it displaced many residents. Socioeconomic changes led to crime and violence for several years. But as Echo Park experienced gentrification at the beginning of the 21st century, new businesses and residents moved in. The now-trendy Echo Park attracts young people to its restaurants, bars, and nightclubs.

Elysian Park is LA's oldest public park. A portion of it is in Echo Park by Dodger Stadium.

Eat!

ECHO PARK CAFÉ
(Valerie Echo Park)
1665 Echo Park Ave.
213-250-9365

EL COMPADRE
1449 W Sunset Blvd.
213-250-4505

MASA OF ECHO PARK
1800 Sunset Blvd.
213-989-1558

PATRA BURGERS
1524 Sunset Blvd.
213-250-0301

TIP

The LA Conservancy offers tours of the late 19th-century neighborhood and LA's best examples of Victorian architecture. The video to Michael Jackson's "Thriller" was filmed here.

laconservancy.org

Visit!

CHAVEZ RAVINE ARBORETUM IN ELYSIAN PARK
929 Academy Rd.
213-485-3287

ECHO PARK LAKE
751 Echo Park Ave.

to Do!

DODGER STADIUM
Take a behind-the-scenes tour and see a game.
1000 Vin Scully Ave.
866-363-4377

BAXTER STREET STAIRS
Over 230 steps lead to views.
2100 Park Dr.

CONTINUE WEST ON SUNSET BOULEVARD in Silver Lake. Turn left on Manzanita Street at Sunset junction. Turn right on Santa Monica Boulevard.

SILVER LAKE

Hilly neighborhoods, twin reservoirs, hidden stairs, indie venues, and a vibrant arts and music scene distinguish Silver Lake, situated in the east-central region of Los Angeles.

The hipster neighborhood attracts artists, creatives, professionals, and young families who can be seen strolling or jogging along Silver Lake and Ivanhoe's 2.2-mile walking path.

The lower lake and the neighborhood were named in 1907 after Herman Silver, who was a city councilman and water commissioner around the turn of the century. But even earlier, around 1887, the area was known as Ivanhoe, named after Sir Walter Scott's book *Ivanhoe*. Francis Marion Smith, a local developer in the late 19th century, was inspired by the book and title character.

Silver Lake's Sunset Junction has dozens of shops and venues along Sunset Boulevard. It's also worth checking out Silver Lake's historic "secret" stairs, which is how residents used to get from their steep hillside homes to main streets to access public transportation before cars were around.

Among the "secret" stairs are the Music Box Steps, made famous by the Laurel and Hardy 1932 short film *The Music Box* (in which they had to carry

TIP

Park the car and climb the Music Box Steps.

a piano up a flight of steep steps between Vendome Street and Descanso Drive). A small Laurel and Hardy Park is at the base of the stairs.

For a more relaxing outing and a bite to eat, visit the Silver Lake Farmers Market, open on Tuesdays and Saturdays.

Eat!

ALIMENTO
1710 Silver Lake Blvd.
323-928-2888

LAMILL COFFEE
1636 Silver Lake Blvd.
323-663-4441

L&E OYSTER BAR
1637 Silver Lake Blvd.
323-660-2255

RED LION TAVERN
German beer garden since 1959.
2366 Glendale Blvd.
323-662-5337

Visit!

LAUREL AND HARDY PARK
(dogs allowed)
3022 Del Monte Dr.

MUSIC BOX STEPS
923 N Vendome St.

SILVERLAKE LOUNGE
2906 Sunset Blvd.
323-741-0032

ZUBULON
Live music venue with a restaurant.
2478 Fletcher Dr.
323-663-6927

Stay!

SILVER LAKE POOL & INN
4141 Santa Monica Blvd.
323-486-7225

to Do!

SILVER LAKE FARMERS MARKET
(Tuesday afternoons and Saturday mornings)
3700 Sunset Blvd.
213-484-4002

The top of Music Box Steps

CONTINUE WEST THROUGH EAST HOLLYWOOD on Santa Monica Boulevard.

EAST HOLLYWOOD

This multicultural neighborhood of about 78,000 residents is part of the Hollywood area in Central LA but has its own distinct character and notable attractions, such as Barnsdall Art Park and Los Angeles City College.

The East Hollywood area began as a farming village in the early 20th century. In 1910, East Hollywood and Hollywood were annexed to the City of LA to tap into the city's water supply. A portion of the neighborhood was called Prospect Park in anticipation of the development of a recreational area. But it was renamed Barnsdall Art Park after Aline Barnsdall, an oil heiress and patron of the arts, who purchased a 36-acre property atop Olive Hill in 1919 to create a destination for the arts in Los Angeles. She commissioned Frank Lloyd Wright to design her residence, named Hollyhock House.

During the 1920s, Armenian immigrants settled in the area that is now Little Armenia. East Hollywood is ethnically diverse with many groups, including Filipino, Japanese, and Thai.

TIP

Take a tour of Hollyhock House, the oldest Frank Lloyd Wright house in LA. It was designed as a garden-style house to integrate the indoors with outdoor gardens.

Eat!

EL ZARAPE TAQUERÍA
5203 Fountain Ave.
323-741-0465

OSTERIA MOZZA
6602 Melrose Ave.
323-297-0100

Visit!

BARNSDALL ART PARK
4800 Hollywood Blvd.

HOLLYHOCK HOUSE
4800 Hollywood Blvd.
323-913-4030

The hilltop Hollyhock House was built between 1918 and 1921.

CONTINUE WEST THROUGH HOLLYWOOD on Santa Monica Boulevard.

The Hollywood Forever Cemetery

HOLLYWOOD

From its humble beginnings as a subdivision in 1887, Hollywood transformed into a popular residential area and world leader in motion picture production in the 1920s. By the 1930s, Hollywood was producing 600 films a year.

Hollywood was laid out as a subdivision by Harvey Wilcox, but it was real estate magnate H. J. Whitley who developed Hollywood into a residential area. Hollywood was incorporated in 1910.

Each year, Hollywood gets over 50 million visitors, making it one of the world's top tourist destinations. By noon each day, Hollywood and Sunset boulevards are packed with tourists who come to see the Hollywood Walk of Fame, TCL Chinese Theatre, and Art Deco–style Pantages Theatre and to experience the Hollywood scene. There's no shortage of museums, theaters, souvenir shops, and restaurants.

Escape the crowds at the Hollywood Forever Cemetery. Established in 1899, it's the area's oldest landmark and final resting place for many notable figures. It also serves as the site for various cultural events. You can also see the hillside Hollywood sign from here.

Interested in movie history? Visit the Hollywood Heritage Museum in the restored 1901 Lasky-DeMille Barn. Exhibits feature photos, historical documents, movie props, and other movie-related memorabilia.

TIP

Scoop up more Hollywood history at the Hollywood Museum in the historic Max Factor building. The museum features iconic stars' dressing rooms, costumes, props, scripts, cars, and thousands of other authentic Hollywood items.

Eat!

MUSSO & FRANK GRILL
6667 Hollywood Blvd.
323-467-7788

PINK'S HOT DOGS
Iconic hot dog stand since 1939.
709 N La Brea Ave.
323-931-4223

Stay!

GODFREY HOTEL
1400 Cahuenga Blvd.
323-380-6111

HOLLYWOOD HOTEL
1160 N Vermont Ave.
323-315-1872

HOLLYWOOD HISTORIC HOTEL
5162 Melrose Ave.
800-555-1333

HOLLYWOOD ROOSEVELT HOTEL (1927)
7000 Hollywood Blvd.
323-466-7000

MAGIC CASTLE HOTEL
7025 Franklin Ave.
323-851-0800

Visit!

EGYPTIAN THEATRE HOLLYWOOD
6712 Hollywood Blvd.
323-306-4302

HOLLYWOOD FOREVER CEMETERY
6000 Santa Monica Blvd.

MAGIC CASTLE
7001 Franklin Ave.
323-851-3313

TCL CHINESE THEATRE
6925 Hollywood Blvd.
323-461-3331

THE HOLLYWOOD MUSEUM
1660 Highland Ave.
323-464-7776

to Do!

HOLLYWOOD BOWL (1922)
2301 Highland Ave.
323-850-2000

HOLLYWOOD WALK OF FAME
Start at Hollywood Blvd. and Highland Ave.

JOHN ANSON FORD THEATER ("THE FORD," 1920)
2580 Cahuenga Blvd.
323-850-2000

PANTAGES THEATRE
Built in 1930 as the last palace theater in Hollywood.
6233 Hollywood Blvd.
323-468-1700

CONTINUE WEST on Santa Monica Boulevard.

WEST HOLLYWOOD

Although West Hollywood (WeHo) attracted creative types early on, it also stands out for its progressive politics and lifestyle.

Since 1984, it's been a self-governed gay city with celebrity-owned restaurants, boutique hotels, and vibrant nightlife in five districts: Sunset Strip, Rainbow, Design, Mid-City, and East Side.

From 1896 to 1924, the town was known as Sherman, named after real estate developer and entrepreneur Moses Hazeltine Sherman. Film stars working in Hollywood flocked to the area. Charlie Chaplin, Mary Pickford, and Douglas Fairbanks established the Pickford-Fairbanks Studio, today known as the Lot.

But the town also attracted other creatives, such as Lloyd Wright (the son of Frank Lloyd Wright), who designed the Lloyd Wright Studio-Residence as his home and workspace in the 1920s.

In 1925, West Hollywood was renamed to better align with Hollywood. A road at

TIP

More time? Visit Miracle Mile, "Museum Row," home to the La Brea Tar Pits & Museum, LA County Museum of Art, Petersen Automotive Museum, and Craft Contemporary Museum.

Stay!

CHAMBERLAIN WEST HOLLYWOOD
1000 Westmount Dr.
310-657-7400

HOTEL ZIGGY
8462 W Sunset Blvd.
323-654-4600

PETIT ERMITAGE
8822 Cynthia St.
310-854-1114

SUNSET MARQUIS
1200 Alta Loma Rd.
310-657-1333

THE CHARLIE
819 N Sweetzer Ave.
323-988-9000

to Do!

BOOK SOUP
8818 Sunset Blvd.
310-659-3110

MAK CENTER FOR ART AND ARCHITECTURE
An art museum and cultural center headquartered in the Shindler House.
835 Kings Rd.
323-651-1510

the northern border of West Hollywood connected Hollywood and Beverly Hills and became known as Sunset Boulevard—the Sunset Strip—with restaurants, hotels, and nightclubs.

West Hollywood evolved into a hip hangout for musicians, artists, and hippies in the 1960s and 1970s. Led Zeppelin, Elton John, and the Doors performed in music venues that included the Troubadour, the Whisky A Go Go, and the Roxy. The Strip was a cultural center for punk rock and New Wave in the late 1970s and heavy metal in the 1980s. Around the same time, gay, lesbian, and genderqueer-identifying people moved to West Hollywood and were instrumental in incorporating the area as the City of West Hollywood in 1984, establishing the area as a trendy and progressive city.

Eat!

AMOUR
8715 Beverly Blvd.
424-431-6717

CASA MADERA
8440 Sunset Blvd.
310-878-0814

CONNIE AND TED'S
8171 Santa Monica Blvd.
323-848-2722

CRAIG'S
8826 Melrose Ave.
310-276-1900

DIALOG CAFÉ
8766 Holloway Dr.
310-289-1630

HARLOWE
Cocktail bar and gastropub fare.
7321 Santa Monica Blvd.
323-876-5839

LAUREL HARDWARE
7984 Santa Monica Blvd.
323-656-6070

MADEO RESTAURANT
8490 Sunset Blvd.
310-859-4903

STRINGS OF LIFE (S.O.L.)
8535 Melrose Ave.
424-313-8136

TAIL O' THE PUP
8512 Santa Monica Blvd.
424-527-0131

THE FORMOSA CAFÉ
7156 Santa Monica Blvd.
323-794-1106

ORIGINAL FARMERS MARKET
(open daily, 9 a.m. to 9 p.m. Monday through Friday, 10 a.m. to 9 p.m. Saturday, 10 a.m. to 7 p.m. Sunday)
6333 W 3rd St. at Fairfax (Mid-City)
323-933-9211

Visit!

THE COMEDY STORE
8433 Sunset Blvd.
323-656-6225

THE VIPER ROOM
(live music venue)
8852 Sunset Blvd.
310-358-1881

TROUBADOUR
9081 N Santa Monica Blvd.

WHISKY A GO GO
Live music venue since 1964, inducted into the Rock and Roll Hall of Fame in 2006.
8901 Sunset Blvd.
310-652-4202

CONTINUE WEST on Santa Monica Boulevard.

BEVERLY HILLS

Beverly Hills is a walkable city with water fountains and green space that span from San Vicente Boulevard to Whittier Drive. Long before Beverly Hills was discovered by Hollywood and the film industry, it was a sought-after community for its water flowing from Franklin, Coldwater, and Benedict canyons. Indigenous people considered this a sacred site and named it Gathering of the Waters.

The birth of today's Beverly Hills began in 1907 when developer Burton Green opened the subdivision. Beverly Hills was incorporated in 1914.

To bring potential home buyers to the area, the Beverly Hills Hotel was built in 1912 and served as the center of community life. Movie stars migrating to the area started a trend of building stylish mansions. Douglas Fairbanks and Mary Pickford built their Pickfair in 1919, and actor/writer Will Rogers was appointed honorary mayor in 1926.

To differentiate Beverly Hills from the City of Los Angeles, eight Beverly Hills city shield signs stand at the city's borders. Easily recognizable is the Golden Triangle, Beverly Hills's central business district and best known for Rodeo Drive, home to high-end boutiques and designer stores.

Beverly Hills also has unique cultural attractions, which include Greystone Mansion and Gardens: Doheny Estate. The once-private 1928 mansion was dedicated as a public park in 1971. The Virginia Robinson Gardens were built in 1911 and served as the residence for Virginia and Harry Robinson (of the Robinson department stores).

Stay!

BEVERLY HILLS HOTEL (1912)
9641 Sunset Blvd.
310-276-2251

BEVERLY WILSHIRE, A FOUR SEASONS HOTEL (1928)
9500 Wilshire Blvd.
310-275-5200

THE BEVERLY HILTON (1955)
9876 Wilshire Blvd.
310-274-7777

The 40-foot-long Beverly Hills sign and lily pond are located in Beverly Gardens Park.

Eat!

FOUNTAIN COFFEE ROOM (1949)
(at the Beverly Hills Hotel)
9641 Sunset Blvd.
310-276-2251

IL PASTAIO
(upscale Italian restaurant)
400 N Cañon Dr.
310-205-5444

LA DOLCE VITA (1966)
9785 S Santa Monica Blvd.
310-278-1845

LAWRY'S THE PRIME RIB
100 N La Cienega Blvd.
310-652-2827

MICKEY FINE PHARMACY & GRILL
433 N Roxbury Dr.
310-273-3868

NATE 'N AL'S (1945)
414 N Beverly Dr.
310-274-0101

THE GRILL ON THE ALLEY
9560 Dayton Ave.
310-276-0615

Visit!

BEVERLY GARDENS PARK (1911)
9439 Santa Monica Blvd.
310-288-2220

BEVERLY CAÑON GARDENS
241 N Beverly Dr.
310-285-2467; 310-285-2408

GOLDEN TRIANGLE/RODEO DRIVE
9800 Wilshire Blvd.

THE SHIELD SIGN
(illuminated at night) at the Beverly Hills Visitor Center
9400 S Santa Monica Blvd.

VIRGINIA ROBINSON GARDENS
1008 Elden Way
310-550-2087

to Do!

BEVERLY HILLS FARMERS' MARKET
Open every Sunday from 9 a.m. to 1 p.m.

GREYSTONE MANSION & GARDENS: DOHENY ESTATE
Free to visit the gardens. Guided tours are offered the first Saturday or Sunday of each month, with timed tickets for $8.
905 Loma Vista Dr.
310-285-6830

CONTINUE WEST
on Santa Monica Boulevard

TIP

On a tour, learn about the eerie history of the 1928 Greystone Mansion and Gardens: Doheny Estate. Five months after homeowner Ned Doheny, his wife, and their five children moved in, he was found shot to death in an apparent murder-suicide by a friend and assistant.

The 1920s Greystone Mansion and Gardens: The Doheny Estate was dedicated as a public park in 1971.

CENTURY CITY

Silent cowboy film star Tom Mix and his producer, William Fox, owner of the Fox Studio Corporation, played crucial roles in the acquisition of Century City. However, neither one lived to see its development.

Television's debut in the consumer market in 1948 was a blow to film studios, which lost much of their audience to home televisions.

The major studios, Warner Bros., Paramount, and Universal, sold their ranches to stay afloat. Edmond Herrscher was hired as director of property development to save Twentieth Century Fox Studio from a financial crisis. He saw the possibility of selling parts of the back lot for business and commercial development and named the area Century City.

Over the past several decades, Century City has become a vibrant city with shopping and businesses. The Century Plaza Hotel opened in 1966 as the centerpiece of Century City. Designed by renowned architect Minoru Yamasaki (who later designed New York's World Trade Center), the 19-story curved hotel faces the fountains on the Avenue of the Stars.

Completed in 1975, the Century Plaza Towers are among the most recognizable buildings in Century City. At 44 stories, they're among the tallest in the city.

Eat!

THE STAND
2000 Avenue of the Stars
310-785-0400

Visit!

CENTURY PLAZA TOWERS
2029 Century Park E

Stay!

CENTURY PARK HOTEL
10330 W Olympic Blvd.
310-553-1000

FAIRMONT CENTURY PLAZA
2025 Avenue of the Stars
310-424-3030

to Do!

CENTURY CITY FARMERS MARKET
(Thursdays, 10 a.m. to 2 p.m.)
10100 CA-2

The twin Century Plaza Towers and Fairmont Century Plaza Hotel.

CONTINUE WEST on Santa Monica Boulevard.

WEST LOS ANGELES

The West Los Angeles region encompasses several cities and neighborhoods, including Westwood, home to Westwood Village and the University of California, Los Angeles (UCLA). The university was established in 1919 on Vermont Avenue and relocated to Westwood in 1929, making this a popular and prestigious college town.

Westwood Village is a lively entertainment, shopping, and dining area. The Fox Village Theater (renamed Regency Village Theatre) was built in 1931, and the Bruin Theater (renamed Regency Bruin Theatre) opened in 1937. The theaters, across the street from each other, were closed in July 2024.

Development of the West LA region began with the arrival of railways, the discovery of oil, and the entertainment industry. The community developed as a residential area at the same time. The opening of the Santa Monica Freeway (I-10) and the San Diego Freeway (I-405) in the 1960s brought more residential and commercial growth, with condominiums and high-rise offices along Wilshire Boulevard, a busy 15-mile thoroughfare from Santa Monica to Downtown LA.

Eat!

GG KITCHEN
11419 Santa Monica Blvd.
310-596-9670

Visit!

BRUIN THEATRE
948 Broxton Ave.

FOWLER MUSEUM AT UCLA
308 Charles E. Young Dr. N
310-825-4361

FRANKLIN D. MURPHY SCULPTURE GARDEN
245 Charles E. Young Dr. E
310-443-7000

HAMMER MUSEUM
10899 Wilshire Blvd.
310-443-7000

CONTINUE WEST on Santa Monica Boulevard. To see the Route 66 terminus at Olympic Boulevard, take Santa Monica Boulevard (via the jog on Manzanita), then go south on Lincoln Boulevard.

SANTA MONICA

Route 66 officially ends at the intersection of Olympic and Lincoln boulevards. Mel's Drive-In stands on the corner and has a mural of Route 66 in the parking lot. Penguin Coffee shop, which opened in 1959, became a dentist's office and is now Mel's Drive-In.

There's a Route 66 sign on the Santa Monica Pier, but it's not the official end.

MORE ROUTE 66 TOWNS

As noted earlier, not all alignments went through all Route 66 towns. The 1932–34 Transitional Alignment for Route 66 bypassed the towns of El Sereno, Eagle Rock and Glassell Park—each of which were on Route 66 during various alignments. Thus, they're included here separately.

El Sereno Middle School

EL SERENO
ROUTE 66 ALIGNMENT (1926–32)

Coming from South Pasadena? Veer west onto Huntington Drive to El Sereno.

El Sereno is among the oldest neighborhoods in Los Angeles. Students at El Sereno Junior School don't have to look far to see one of the area's oldest structures. It's in their backyard—or rather their playground.

The Queen Anne Revival–style Farmdale Schoolhouse was built in 1894 to serve the small, rural community of Farmdale (later renamed El Sereno). It's the town's only National Register of Historic Places landmark, added in 2022. In 1975, it was moved to its current location at the northern end of El Sereno Middle School.

TIP

Park on Gambier Street to see the historic Farmdale Schoolhouse on the campus of El Sereno Middle School.

Suburban development in El Sereno began in the 20th century with the expansion of the Pacific Electric Railway, which connected neighborhoods within LA.

El Sereno's population grew during the wartime years 1939–45 as new residents came to work at the aircraft and munitions factories in LA.

Newland Hardware Store, which opened in 1926 (4938 Huntington Drive South), is the longest-operating business in the community. Now called Newland True Value, it is part of the True Value brand. The family has expanded to locations in Altadena and Newhall.

Visit!

EL SERENO LIBRARY
5226 Huntington Dr. S
323-225-9201

FARMDALE SCHOOLHOUSE
(at El Sereno Junior High)
2839 N Eastern Ave.

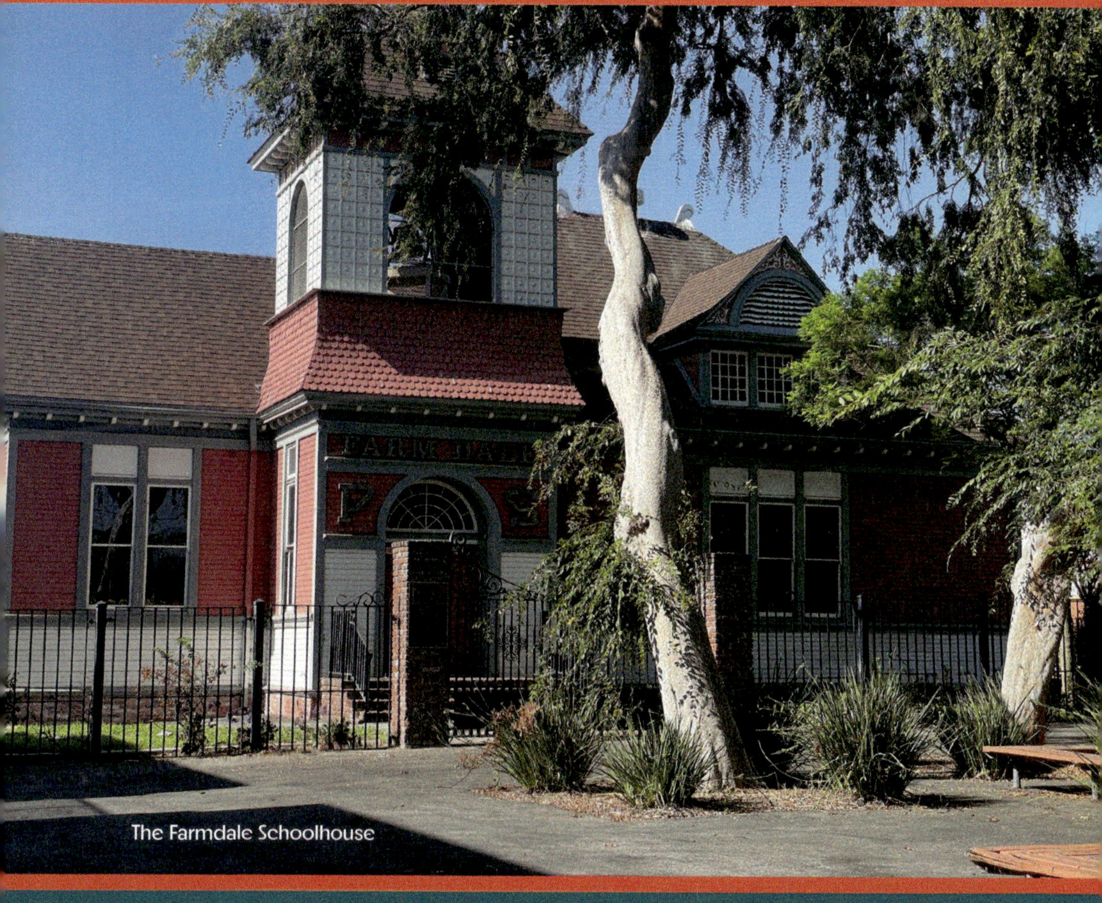

The Farmdale Schoolhouse

ROUTE 66 TRAVELED through Eagle Rock along Colorado Boulevard and Eagle Rock Boulevard from 1934 to 1936. From Pasadena, drive west on Colorado Boulevard over Colorado Street Bridge to Eagle Rock.

Shadow of the eagle on Eagle Rock

EAGLE ROCK

Settlers named the town after a large rock that, depending on where you're standing, has an indentation and shadow that resembles an eagle.

The large sandstone formation, the result of hot springs activity millions of years ago, is situated on the northeastern edge of town. Eagle Rock was developed when Rancho San Rafael was subdivided in 1870 and incorporated in 1911. But by 1923, the need for a steady supply of water forced the city to accept annexation by Los Angeles.

Even though the city declared the eagle-shaped rock a Historic-Cultural Monument in 1962, the rock itself didn't actually belong to Los Angeles until 1995. Initially, the land was owned by developer Fredric Heim, who wanted to build an apartment building at the base of the rock. Residents pushed back, and eventually the city purchased the property for $699,000. That area is now part of Richard Alatorre Park, where there's a one-mile loop trail (Eagle Rock Canyon Trail).

TIP

For the best views of the eagle on the rock, park at the end of the street on 5499 Eagle Rock View Dr.

Locals embrace their Route 66 status and rally to preserve historic places, including the Jay Risk Standard Oil Service Station, a 14-foot-wide gas station built in 1919 in downtown LA and moved to its current site in 1931. It's easy to miss the tiny structure with missing windows that's crammed between buildings in the 1600 block of Colorado Boulevard.

Residential neighborhoods reflect the diverse population and architecture, which include Craftsman, Spanish Colonial Revival, and mid-century modern homes that are surrounded by coffee houses, vintage shops, diners, and craft beer venues.

Eat!

CASA BIANCA (1955)
(pizza)
1650 Colorado Blvd.
323-256-9617

THE FABLE
1630 Colorado Blvd.
323-508-5058

CINDY'S
1500 Colorado Blvd.
323-257-7375

LITTLE BEAST
(situated in a 1911 Craftsman bungalow)
1496 Colorado Blvd.
323-341-5899

Visit!

EAGLE ROCK
(at Richard Alatorre Park)
Park at the end of the cul-de-sac for the best views and photos.
5499 Eagle Rock View Dr.

THE CENTER FOR THE ARTS
(historical society)
2225 Colorado Blvd.
323-561-3044

The 14-foot-wide Jay Risk Standard Oil Service Station built in 1919

GLASSELL PARK

ROUTE 66 ALIGNMENT (1934–36)

This Los Angeles neighborhood dates to the early 20th century, when Andrew Glassell, an attorney and descendant of a prominent California family, purchased land in the area. He and his family built a Victorian home in 1889 and planted citrus orchards and a walnut grove on their numerous acres.

He envisioned a suburban development and began subdividing the land around 1907. During the Depression, the Glassells sold a 62-acre parcel that became Forest Lawn Memorial Park in neighboring Glendale.

The City of LA annexed Glassell Park in stages between 1912 and 1916.

Around this time, the area transitioned from agricultural land and hunting cabins from the 19th century to more subdivided lots. In the 1920s, the Taylor Yard was established, while houses were built in Colonial Revival architecture.

Businesses such as the Peking Noodle Company opened their doors in Glassell Park and in surrounding neighborhoods, including El Monte, an incorporated city. The noodle-making company has been operating since 1924. La Morenita Bakery was established in 1953.

In 1936, the Glassells lost their house to the City of LA by eminent domain for the purpose of building Washington Irving Junior High School. The Glassells received $25,000 as compensation.

Eat!

LA MORENITA BAKERY (1953)
(pan dulce)
11230 Garvey Ave.
626-452-9339

Visit!

RIO DE LOS ANGELES STATE PARK
1900 N San Fernando Rd.

ROUTE 66 DESTINATIONS

A portion of Route 66 travels through the San Gabriel Valley. Sierra Madre, an incorporated city, and Altadena, an unincorporated community, just miss being on Route 66. But they're close and worth including on a road trip.

SIERRA MADRE

Sierra Madre is a charming town encompassing three square miles between Pasadena and Arcadia. It just missed being on Route 66. The historic route's 1926–38 alignment traveled just south of the city limits, and then bypassed Sierra Madre in 1938 when it realigned farther south along Colorado Boulevard.

Sierra Madre was founded in 1881 by Nathaniel Carter, who purchased 1,103 acres and developed the town. It incorporated as a city in 1907.

Jeff Ward, fourth-generation owner of Ward Ranch

Over the next 10 years, the town continued to grow with a new schoolhouse, churches, a library, and town hall.

Edwin Waldo Ward Sr., who was among the earliest residents, purchased 10 acres and planted navel oranges. He

Lizzie's Trail Inn (once owned by Elizabeth "Lizzie" Stoppel) and the Richardson House (hand-built by John Richardson) are now museums.

later acquired another 20 acres and built a barn in 1902 and a Victorian home in 1903. He experimented with recipes, and in 1917 he opened E. Waldo Ward & Son and sold marmalades. The company—the oldest surviving business in Sierra Madre—is in the hands of the fourth generation and sells a variety of jams, spreads, jellies, stuffed olives, and more.

Sierra Madre has several historic structures: Hotel Shirley (1911), Old North Church (1890), Lizzie's Trail Inn (1900), and Richardson House (1890).

FUN FACT: In April 1894, Alice Brugman purchased a wistaria plant in a one-gallon pot for 75 cents. Now the vine covers about one acre and is listed as the world's largest blossoming plant by the Guinness Book of World Records. The public can see it at the Annual Wistaria Festival in spring. sierramadrechamber.com

to Do!

See a live show at the 99-seat **SIERRA MADRE PLAYHOUSE**, which debuted in 1910 and retains its movie theater facade.
87 W Sierra Madre Blvd.
626-355-4318

Eat!

CASA DEL REY
31 N Baldwin Ave.
626-355-6060

CORFU
48 W Sierra Madre Blvd.
626-355-5993

NANO CAFÉ
322 W Sierra Madre Blvd.
626-325-3334

THE ONLY PLACE IN TOWN
Opened in 1945 as the Headline and renamed by Sierra Madre residents.
110 W Sierra Madre Blvd.
626-355-3502

Visit!

HOTEL SHIRLEY (1911)
A restored building that's home to businesses
28 N Baldwin Ave.

LIZZIE'S TRAIL INN AND THE RICHARDSON HOUSE MUSEUMS
167 E Mira Monte Ave.
626-355-3905

OLD NORTH CHURCH
191 W Sierra Madre Blvd.

WARD RANCH
273 E Highland Ave.
626-355-1218

TIP

Stop by Ward Ranch and visit the store (the family's former canning space) behind the main house. The family sells homemade jams from fruit grown on the property.

ALTADENA

Altadena is a scenic community surrounded by wilderness on three sides (the Angeles National Forest, the Arroyo Seco, and Eaton Canyon) and the City of Pasadena on the other.

Situated in an unincorporated area of LA County, Altadena is a diverse, close-knit community home to outdoor enthusiasts, artists, and those seeking a balance between urban and rural life. Black residents who found refuge in Altadena during the Civil Rights era helped shape the community's identity. Several prominent people helped establish Altadena, founded in 1887. The Mount Wilson Observatory is named after Benjamin Davis Wilson, the second mayor of LA, who acquired land in 1859. His daughter Ruth and her husband, George Smith Patton Sr., had a son, George Patton Jr., who became a decorated WWII general.

Benjamin S. Eaton also played a role in shaping the area. Eaton Canyon, a popular natural area, is named after him.

About 30 years later, brothers John and Frederick Woodbury developed much of the land that became Altadena. Thinking outside the box was inventor Thaddeus Sobieski Lowe, founder of the Mount Lowe Railway, which traveled from Altadena to the top of Mount Echo from 1893 to

The Bunny Museum burned to the ground in the January 2025 wildfires but the owners plan to rebuild in the same location.

1938. While it was a popular tourist attraction, maintanence costs and natural disasters, including fires and floods, eventually shut down the railway.

Altadena has had several catastrophic events. In 1918, Charles Cobb, a retired lumber magnate, and his wife, Carrie, built a Spanish-themed mansion on land that was formerly the site of an unsuccessful gold mine. Over the next decades, the estate survived brush fires, plans for a cemetery, and ownership by the Marx Brothers before it was turned into public parkland owned by the US Forest Service. The area is said to be haunted.

In January 2025, wildfires destroyed thousands of structures in Altadena. Among them: Fox's Restaurant, the Andrew McNally House (the former home of the cofounder and president of Rand McNally publishing company), the Zane Grey Estate, and houses along Christmas Tree Lane Monument, a historic district since 1920. The Bunny Museum, which contained thousands of bunny-themed collectibles, also burned, but the owners say they plan to rebuild.

Eat!

AMARA KITCHEN
841 E Mariposa St.
626-365-1633

EL PATRON
2555 Lake Ave.
626-296-2818

PIZZA OF VENICE
2545 N Fair Oaks Ave.
626-765-9636

BULGARINI
749 E Altadena Dr.
626-791-6174

EVEREST
2314 Lake Ave.
626-797-8204

Visit!

BUNNY MUSEUM
A private collection of an assortment of bunny-themed collectibles.
2605 Lake Ave.
626-798-8848
thebunnymuseum.com

TIP

Take a hike on the Sam Merrill Trail, which starts at the Cobb Estate: 3302 Lake Avenue.

Cobb Estate and Sam Merrill Trailhead

PACIFIC
CREST
NATL
ANGELES
NATIONAL
FOREST
SAN GABRIEL MTS.
Creek
TRAIL
REC.
ANGELES FOREST HWY
TUJUNGA
RD
LITTLE
CANYON RD
BIG TUJUNGA
Alder
Strawberry Peak
6,164
NATL
SCENIC
NATL
FOOTHILL
Hansen L.
Sunland-Tujugna
FRWY
FOOTHILL BL
ANGELES
CREST
NATL
REC.
TRAIL
MOCCASIN
GABRIELINO
VERDUGO MTS.
La Crescenta
Montrose
La Cañada Flintridge
Mt. Wilson
5,710
Burbank
Glendale
Altadena
170
NORTH HOLLYWOOD
210
Sierra Madre
Pasadena
VENTURA
FRWY
134
STUDIO CITY
134
Griffith Park
5
EAGLE ROCK
HOLLYWOOD
South Pasadena
San Marino
DR
101
West
110
Alhambra
San Gabriel
HUNTINGTON
2
19
Rosemead
El Monte
Beverly Hills
5
Monterey Park
Whittier Narrows Reg. Rec. Area
South El Monte
10
710
S. San Gabriel
60
10
60
E. Los Angeles
187
Culver City
View Park
Vernon
Windsor Hills
Huntington Park
90
Ladera Hts.
19
Pico Rivera
Inglewood
Florence
Bell
710
Bell Gdns.
Walnut Park
Cudahy
110
5
Santa Fe Springs
South Gate
Athens
Lennox
105
Lynwood
S. Whittier
IMPERIAL

FOOTHILL BOULEVARD

Foothill Boulevard is a major thoroughfare in LA that travels 60 miles from San Bernardino to Sylmar. In San Gabriel Valley, Foothill Boulevard is Route 66.

Foothill Boulevard also travels through most of the Crescenta Valley, situated between the Verdugo Mountains and the foothills of Angeles National Forest. This area comprises the LA city communities of La Cañada Flintridge, La Crescenta-Montrose, and a portion of the City of Glendale to Sunland and Tujunga.

Although Foothill Boulevard is no longer Route 66 in Crescenta Valley, locals consider Foothill to be their Main Street. It travels through La Cañada, La Crescenta,Tujunga, and Sunland. Although it doesn't veer into adjacent Montrose, there is a turnoff from La Cañada down Verdugo Boulevard that leads to Honolulu Boulevard in Montrose.

Historically, Foothill Boulevard began as a surveyor's line in the late 1870s, around the time when people were drawn to the valley's healthful climate. Sanitariums and health resorts were common. In the 1920s, the valley became semirural with ranchers growing citrus, stone fruit, and grapes.

After WWII, Crescenta Valley developed into a suburb with distinctive communities from affluent La Canada Flintridge to rustic Sunland-Tujunga.

In January 1952, the City of Glendale annexed the strip that included the commercial section of Montrose. The communities of La Cañada and Flintridge joined together in incorporation in December 1976, while portions of La Crescenta and Montrose remain as part of Los Angeles County.

TO START THE TOUR, **BEGIN IN LA CAÑADA FLINTRIDGE** and follow Foothill Boulevard through Crescenta Valley. **OR,** start in neighboring Glendale, then drive to La Cañada Flintridge.

A Gladding McBean statue, *Reclining Nude*, is known as Rockhaven's symbol—the Lady of Rockhaven

DETOUR

GLENDALE

Glendale encompasses 34 neighborhoods that are divided by streets, washes, and mountain ridges.

In the late 1700s, Glendale—along with neighboring Highland Park, Eagle Rock, and Burbank—was part of the original Rancho San Rafael. The rancho was eventually dissolved, and after Glendale's incorporation in 1906, it grew steadily through numerous annexations. It's an ethnically diverse city with a population of 183,000, of which about 40 percent are Armenians.

Among Glendale's most notable landmarks is the Brand Library and Art Center, the former home (named Miradero) of Glendale pioneer Leslie Coombs Brand, who was instrumental in the development of Glendale in the early 1900s.

When Brand died in 1925, he bequeathed his estate to the City of Glendale upon the death of his wife (1945), provided the property be turned into a public library and park. A trail leads to the Brand Family Cemetery, which is marked by a pyramid. On the grounds is the Doctors House Museum, one of Glendale's two remaining Queen Anne–Eastlake style Victorian homes. Built in 1888, it was occupied in succession by four notable doctors, hence the name.

Downtown's Brand Boulevard is a lively main street with restaurants, stores, and the historic Alex Theatre, built in 1925. After it fell into disrepair in the 1980s, it was renovated and reopened in the 1990s as a performing arts and entertainment venue.

Glendale is also known for mega malls: the Glendale Galleria and the Americana at Brand.

TIP

Check for occasional tours at Rockhaven, owned by the City of Glendale.
friendsofrockhaven.org
2713 Honolulu Ave.
747-688-0311

Eat!

PHO 22
2230 Honolulu Ave.
818-957-2121

THE BLACK COW
2219 Honolulu Ave.
818-957-5282

Visit!

ADAMS SQUARE MINI PARK GAS STATION
Built in 1936 by Richfield Oil Corporation and unused since the 1980s, it's an example of a streamline moderne gas station.
1020 E Palmer Ave.
818-548-2864

MUSEUM OF NEON ART
216 S Brand Blvd.
818-696-2149

CASA ADOBE DE SAN RAFAEL
Built in 1865, it's one of the oldest homes in Glendale. There's a museum and picnic grounds.
1330 Dorothy Dr.
818-548-2184

DOCTORS HOUSE MUSEUM AND GAZEBO
(at Brand Library)
1692 Brand Park Dr.
818-548-3782

ROCKHAVEN SANITARIUM HISTORIC DISTRICT
2713 Honolulu Ave.
747-688-0311

Stay!

GLENDALE HOTEL
1510 E Colorado St.
818-507-6688

GLENRIDGE INN
1437 E Colorado St.
818-246-8367

GRIFFITH PARK MOTEL
1634 Victory Blvd.
818-244-5071

BRAND PLAZA HOTEL
339 ½ N Brand Blvd.
818-244-3820

to Do!

ALEX THEATRE
216 N Brand Blvd.
818-254-8456

BRAND LIBRARY & ART CENTER
1601 W Mountain St.
818-548-2051

GRIFFITH OBSERVATORY
2800 E Observatory Rd.
213-473-0800

GRIFFITH PARK
Over 4,200 acres with picnic areas, hiking trails, and attractions like the Los Angeles Zoo and the Autry Museum.
Between Los Feliz Blvd. on the south and Ventura Freeway (134) on the north

TAKE THE VENTURA FREEWAY (134 East) to the Glendale Freeway (2 North). Exit toward Foothill Boulevard. It's about a 10-minute drive.

Historic Lanterman House

LA CAÑADA FLINTRIDGE

This affluent suburban city is the gateway to the Angeles National Forest. It was founded in the early 1870s by homesteaders, and the Lanterman family was among the first settlers who put down roots, in 1875. The family's son, Dr. Roy Lanterman, and his wife lived in a 1915 Mexican Colonial hacienda. Today, that property is the historic Lanterman House, which is open for public tours by appointment.

Many of the early settlers arrived seeking a healthy climate for family members with tuberculosis or bronchitis. Around 1893, there were 53 houses in La Cañada. Most were ranchers struggling with drought and economic challenges.

Visit!

CHERRY CANYON PARK
4171 Cherry Canyon Motorway

LANTERMAN HOUSE
4420 Encinas Dr.
818-790-1421

JET PROPULSION LABORATORY
Free public tours are available with advance reservations.
4800 Oak Grove Dr.
818-354-4321

NEWCOMB'S RANCH
a historic roadhouse (currently closed)
CA-2

Eat!

BERGE'S SANDWICHES
1044 Foothill Blvd. #3222
818-790-2422

to Do!

Explore the 150-acre **DESCANSO GARDENS'** themed gardens, ponds, and forested areas.
1418 Descanso Dr.
818-949-4200

FLINTRIDGE RIDING CLUB
4625 Oak Grove Dr.
818-952-1233

TIP

This is the perfect place to start the Angeles Crest Highway tour through the Angeles National Forest. The closest picnic area is Switzer Picnic Site and Falls. Or keep going to reach the larger Charleton Flats picnic area.

La Cañada's somewhat remote location makes it an ideal setting for the Jet Propulsion Laboratory (JPL), founded in 1936 by Caltech researchers. JPL is the leading US center for robotic exploration of the solar system. Owned by NASA, the 168-acre JPL campus is mostly located in La Cañada but uses a Pasadena mailing address.

In 1976, the communities of La Cañada and Flintridge merged and incorporated as a General Law City.

Descanso Gardens

FROM FOOTHILL, GO WEST ON VERDUGO Boulevard, which turns into Honolulu Avenue in Montrose.

LA CRESCENTA-MONTROSE

Although the two communities share a hyphenated name they're uniquely different—yet complement each other well.

Montrose is a shopping area populated with mom-and-pop eateries and stores along Honolulu Avenue. It has a Mayberry town vibe. No wonder Crescenta Valley residents like to gather here for a meal or coffee and festive events.

Named after Honolulu, Hawaii, by developers, Honolulu Avenue is the heart of Montrose and where the first commercial building opened in 1914 at Honolulu Avenue and Verdugo Road. The year before, realtor Robert A. Walton and investor J. Frank Walters hosted a barbecue and began selling lots for the new town.

By the 1920s, Montrose was growing rapidly with the opening of a pharmacy, hotel, theater, bank, and retail stores. Growth slowed during the Great Depression but picked up after WWII.

Visit!

ONCE UPON A TIME BOOKSTORE
2207 Honolulu Ave.
818-248-9668

to Do!

MONTROSE BOWL
Retro bowling alley since 1940 with restaurant.
2334 Honolulu Ave.
818-253-5969

Portions of Montrose were annexed by the neighboring city of Glendale between 1951 and 1955. But when local politicians considered turning Honolulu Avenue into a truck route, local merchants banded together to create the Montrose Shopping Park in 1967. The City of Glendale designated Montrose as Glendale's official Old Town.

TIP

Shop for books at Once Upon a Time Bookstore, the oldest bookstore in the county. It opened in 1966 and is owned by the hands-on Palacios family.

Eat!

ALISSA'S OCEAN VIEW BAR & GRILL
3826 Ocean View Blvd.
818-248-2722

BLUE FISH JAPANESE RESTAURANT
(sushi bar)
2261 Honolulu Ave.
818-248-9700

CASA CÓRDOBA
2331 Honolulu Ave.
818-937-4445

GIUSEPPE'S PIZZERIA
2428 Honolulu Ave.
747-255-7402

GUS & ANDY'S
2201 Honolulu Ave.
818-415-4756

JOSELITO'S
(Mexican)
2345 Honolulu Ave.
818-957-1901

PEPE'S
(Mexican)
2272 Honolulu Ave.
818-248-6622

SEASONING ALLEY
2332 Honolulu Ave.
818-249-4949

THEE ELBOW ROOM
2418 Honolulu Ave.
818-248-1769

TOWN KITCHEN & GRILL
2276 Honolulu Ave.
818-248-1881

VALEU ESPETOS
(Brazilian)
2232 Honolulu Ave.
818-369-7277

FOLLOW HONOLULU AVENUE WEST to Verdugo City.

VERDUGO CITY

Verdugo City is a bit of a mystery. There's a sign for it on the 210 Freeway, and its name is included in community organization names like the Montrose-Verdugo City Chamber of Commerce and the Montrose-Sparr Heights-Verdugo City Neighborhood Association. There's even a Verdugo City Post Office (at La Crescenta and Honolulu) with its own zip code: 91046. But technically, the post office is Verdugo City. That zip code is valid only for

Verdugo City Post Office

post office boxes within the post office itself. The demographics of that zip code show a population of zero.

Yet Verdugo City is one of Glendale's historic neighborhoods. It even has a little blue sign designating it as such.

According to local historians Mike Morgan and Mike Lawler, Verdugo City comprises about 10 acres, roughly bordered by La Crescenta Avenue to the east, Montrose Avenue to the north, Ramsdell to the west, and the Verdugo Mountains to the south.

Verdugo City was created by real estate developer Harry Fowler in 1923. His dream was to create a new town in the unincorporated Crescenta Valley, specifically at the intersection of Crescenta Avenue and Honolulu, where a car and bus route then ran between Glendale and Tujunga.

He built the post office and the grand two-story brick Fowler Building, where a Chevron station stands today. The Fowler Building had a pharmacy and soda fountain on the first floor, and offices and an event space upstairs. The Fowler Building was destroyed in the 1971 earthquake. However, the Fowler Building's architectural style may be adopted for a new Trader Joe's Montrose branch.

GO WEST ON HONOLULU AVENUE to Pennsylvania Avenue. At Foothill you are in the split between incorporated (turn west) and unincorporated (turn east) La Crescenta.

LA CRESCENTA-MONTROSE

Although Montrose lies mostly within the City of Glendale, La Crescenta locals proudly consider Montrose part of their community. It's understandable, since both are laid-back, family-friendly communities with mom-and-pop businesses. But La Crescenta has a longer history.

The first American settler to La Crescenta was Theodore Pickens, in 1871. But Benjamin B. Briggs is credited with establishing La Crescenta, which was known for its healthy climate to treat lung disease. Briggs, a physician from Indiana, settled in La Crescenta in 1882 and bought a parcel of land from Pickens. He platted and recorded the Crescenta Cañada tracts and created the townsite of Crescenta in 1884. That same year, the town was renamed La Crescenta by the post office to distinguish it from Crescent City.

La Crescenta was primarily agricultural land until after WWII, when housing tracts replaced farms. In the 1970s, the opening of the 210 Freeway (which locals unsuccessfully fought) led to the urbanization of La Crescenta as part of Greater Los Angeles. Yet La Crescenta retains its small-town vibe and cherishes its history.

St. Luke's of the Mountains church, which was built with stones from Angeles National Forest, is a community gathering place.

One of its oldest organizations is the La Crescenta Woman's Club, a community service group that formed as the Crescenta Club in 1907. It officially became La Crescenta Woman's Club in 1911, and still meets in the clubhouse built in 1925.

Another beloved landmark is St. Luke's of the Mountains, designed and built by artist Seymour Thomas in 1924. The beautiful church features stained glass, native stone, and massive chimes that ring throughout La Crescenta.

FUN FACT: Immigrant French winemaker George Le Mesnager planted thousands of grapevines in La Crescenta in 1885. At that time, the wine industry was booming in LA. Le Mesnager had a winery near Downtown LA.

Around 1910, Le Mesnager's son, Louis, built a stone barn for storage, livestock, and living quarters. The stone barn and vineyards have been owned by the City of Glendale since 1986.

SUNLAND–TUJUNGA

As you drive along Foothill Boulevard, you'll notice the changing landscape from the manicured lawns of La Cañada–Flintridge and La Crescenta to the more rural neighborhoods in Sunland and Tujunga. The twin communities began as separate settlements around 1880. Sunland was annexed to the City of Los Angeles in 1926, and Tujunga in 1932. The two communities merged under a hyphenated name in 1928 and share a police station, branch library, city council, and high school.

Foothill Boulevard is the main roadway and where most businesses are located. Tujunga

TIP

Take a side trip on Big Tujunga Canyon Road, which runs from the Sunland area at Oro Vista Avenue to Angeles Forest Highway. It passes campgrounds and a flood control reservoir. This road is used by commuters heading from the Antelope Valley to LA during the week.

Big Tujunga Canyon Road was also the birthplace of the Hog Farm, the longest-running hippie commune and the campsite of Eden Ahbez, a proto hippie in the 1950s who wrote "Nature Boy," an early hit for Nat King Cole.

Visit!

CRESCENTA VALLEY HIGH SCHOOL
(built in 1933 as a junior high school)
2900 Community Ave.

LA CRESCENTA WOMAN'S CLUB
4004 La Crescenta Ave.

LE MESNAGER BARN
The stone barn is located in Deukmejian Wilderness Park, 3429 Markridge Rd, Glendale

ST. LUKE'S OF THE MOUNTAINS
2563 Foothill Blvd.
818-248-3639

Eat!

TICKLE TREE CAFÉ
2853 Foothill Blvd.
818-249-4169

Stay!

LA CRESCENTA MOTEL
2413 Foothill Blvd.
818-248-1294

DRIVE WEST ON FOOTHILL BOULEVARD to Sunland-Tujunga.

Canyon Boulevard is another primary roadway but is mostly residential.

For historical places of interest, drive to Bolton Hall Museum. It was built in 1913 as a community center and today serves as a museum with exhibits depicting local history.

Eat!

JOSELITO'S MEXICAN FOOD TUJUNGA
7308 Foothill Blvd.
818-951-2275

MI CASITA
8069 Foothill Blvd.
818-352-5250

THE BACK DOOR BAKERY & CAFÉ
8349 Foothill Blvd.
818-353-2233

Visit!

BOLTON HALL MUSEUM
10110 Commerce Ave.
818-352-3420

Bolton Hall Museum

TIP

Buy a National Forest Adventure Pass to park in a picnic or hiking area. Get an early start, because parking lots fill up quickly. Switzer Picnic Area is the first one you'll pass, followed by Charlton Flats and Chaleo. Although currently closed, the 1939 Newcomb's Ranch roadhouse is still a popular rest stop. There are also several vista points with mountain and valley views.

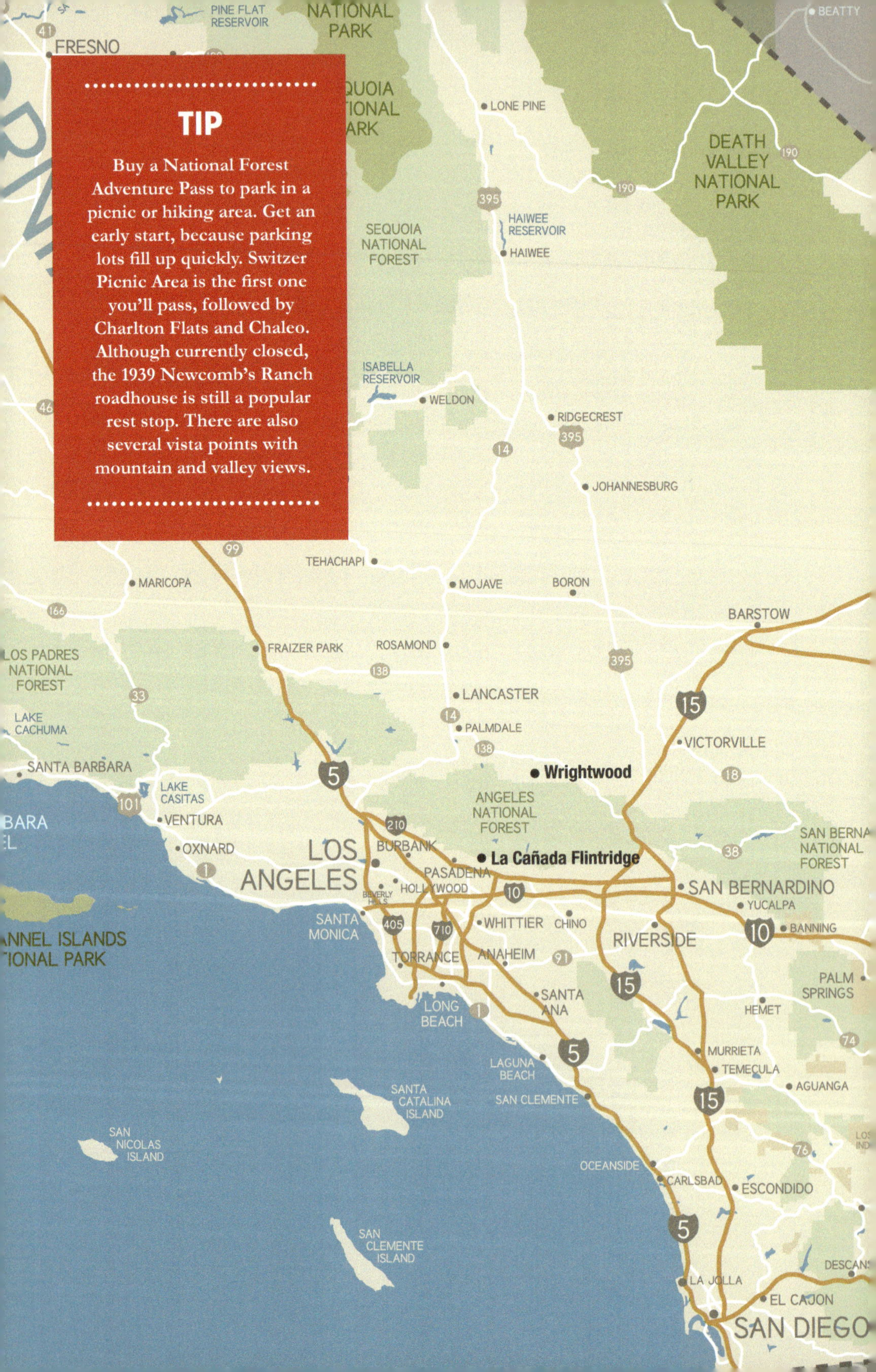

ANGELES CREST HIGHWAY

Proximity to Angeles National Forest, in the San Gabriel Mountains, makes this area a favorite getaway for Angelenos. It's reachable via Angeles Crest Highway (State Route 2), a scenic 66-mile highway that winds through the pine forest from the residential community of La Cañada Flintridge to the mountain town of Wrightwood.

The two-lane Angeles Crest Highway is both a National Forest Scenic Byway and a designated California Scenic Highway. It was completed in 1956.

Although you won't find towns along the highway, there are several picnic areas, campgrounds, visitor centers, and hiking trails. Top sites include the historic Mt. Wilson Observatory, Charleton Flats picnic area, and the Chilao Visitor Center. In winter, skiers flock to Mt. Waterman, a small resort along the highway.

Winter also brings storms and road closures due to snow, rockfall, and avalanche hazards. However, it's a beautiful road to travel in spring, summer, and fall when you can enjoy the changing seasons and pine-scented air.

Covering about 700,000 acres, Angeles National Forest was the first national forest in California and the second in the United States. It's the largest urban forest in the US. Elevations range up to 10,064 feet at Mt. San Antonio (best known as Mt. Baldy). Angeles National Forest was created by proclamation of President Benjamin Harrison in 1892. It was originally called San Gabriel Timberland Reserve and changed to San Gabriel National Forest in 1907. On July 1, 1908, the name was changed to Angeles National Forest.

START THIS TOUR IN

LA CAÑADA FLINTRIDGE
off the 210 Freeway.

Courtesy of Mountain High Resorts

WRIGHTWOOD

Accessible from Angeles Crest Highway and Pearblossom Highway (Route 138)

This quaint mountain's accessibility from LA (about a 90-minute drive) makes it an enjoyable year-round resort, but it's especially popular in winter for skiing and snowboarding at Mountain High. Yeti's Snow Parks round out fun snow activities. Mountain High encompasses three separate mountains—East, West, and North Resorts.

But skiing wasn't the original plan. Sumner Wright, who arrived in the mountain area in the late 1800s, acquired land to develop a cattle ranch—the Circle Mountain Cattle Company—during the early 1900s. He planted apple trees and raised trotting horses.

After a downswing in the cattle industry, he sold off lots for summer resort residences. Winter sports put Wrightwood on the map. Big Pines debuted in 1924 and became a world-class ski jump five years later. The addition of ski tows and chairlifts in the late 1930s and early 1940s made the area popular for skiing.

In 1941 Blue Ridge Ski Area (now Mountain High West) was developed on the former slopes of Big Pines Park. The ski area was bought and renamed Mountain High in 1975.

Holiday Hill (now Mountain High East) was developed in 1948. Holiday Hill and Mountain High merged when Orange County businessman Terry Tognazzini acquired the resorts. Over the next 18 years, Mountain High became one of Southern California's leading winter resorts. Since then, the Mountain High Ski Area has changed ownership and remains a popular resort for skiing, snowboarding, and snow tubing.

TIP

Nearby Big Pines Recreation Area has 10 campgrounds, five picnic areas, and hiking trails—including a portion of the Pacific Crest Trail.

Eat!

GRIZZLY CAFÉ
1455 State Hwy. 2
760-249-6733

MEXICO LINDO
1253 Evergreen Rd.
760-249-4100

THE EVERGREEN CAFÉ & RACOON SALOON
1269 Evergreen Rd.
760-249-6393

Stay!

CANYON CREEK INN
6059 Pine St.
760-249-4800

CEDAR LODGE MOTEL
5995 Cedar St.
760-249-5062

GRAND PINE CABINS
6045 Pine St.
833-354-1785

to Do!

MOUNTAIN HIGH RESORT
24510 State Hwy. 2
888-754-7878

MOUNTAINEER DAYS
Celebrates Wrightwood's early days with axe-throwing competitions, a parade, and pony rides in July.

SPRING FLING!
Features beer and wine, games, live music, and a car show in early May.

WRIGHTWOOD MOUNTAIN HOLIDAY CELEBRATION
Features a Parade of Lights in November.

CHAMBER OF COMMERCE
760-249-4320

Newhall
Placerita Canyon State Park
ANGELES NATIONAL FOREST
SAN G
Hidden Springs
SANTA SUSANA MTS.
Oat Mtn. 3,747
Omelveny Park
Sylmar
San Fernando
RONALD REAGAN FRWY
GRANADA HILLS
Pacoima
Hansen L.
FOOTHILL
SUNLAND
Chatsworth
SAN FERNANDO VALLEY
NORDHOFF
NORTHRIDGE
La Crescenta
Montrose
La Caña
Canoga Park
Burbank
Verdugo City
Reseda
Ahmanson Ranch
Sepulveda Dam Rec Area
North Hollywood
Glendale
Tarzana
Encino
Woodland Hills
Los Encinos State Hist. Park
Toluca Lake
VENTURA
Encino Reservoir
Sherman Oaks
Studio City
Universal City
Calabasas
Laurel Canyon
Griffith Park
Eagle Roc
Glenview
Topanga State Park
Los Angeles
Hollywood
South Pasade
Monte Nido
West Hollywood
Bel Air
Topanga
Fernwood
MONICA MTS.
Will Rogers State Historic Park
Beverly Hills
Pacific Palisades
Will Rogers State Beach
Malibu
Santa Monica
Santa Monica State Beach
E. Los Angeles
Culver City
View Park
Vernon
Venice
Windsor Hills
Huntington Park
Marina del Rey
Ladera Hts.
WESTCHESTER
Inglewood
Florence
Walnut Park
Cudah
Santa Monica Bay
South Gate
Playa del Rey
Lennox
Athens
Lynwood
El Segundo
Lawndale
Paramount
Manhattan Beach
Hermosa Beach
Redondo Beach
Torrance
Carson
PACIFIC COAST HWY
PACIFIC OCEAN
Palos Verdes Estates
Lomita
Signal Hill
Wilmington
Long Beach
Palos Verdes Point
Rolling Hills
Rancho Palos Verdes
Point Vicente
San Pedro
San Pedro Bay
Point Fermin

PACIFIC COAST HIGHWAY

Pacific Coast Highway (also called Highway 1) is the longest and most scenic state route in California. It's no wonder people come from all over to breathe in the ocean air and soak up the coastal views.

Plans for a scenic coastal route in California began in 1911, but construction took place in phases and was completed in 1937.

Pacific Coast Highway (PCH) travels 656 miles between Dana Point in Orange County and Leggett in Mendocino County. About 41 miles travel through LA County from Long Beach to Malibu. While most of PCH hugs the coastline of the Pacific Ocean, the road turns inland for a few miles (no ocean views) and even changes names in the South Bay.

From Long Beach, PCH zigzags through the South Bay cities of Wilmington, Torrance, Redondo Beach, and Hermosa Beach. In Manhattan Beach, it becomes Sepulveda Boulevard and then turns back to PCH through El Segundo. Then it becomes Lincoln Boulevard from Playa del Rey to Santa Monica, where you turn left at Lincoln and Olympic Boulevards. There's a sign for PCH North on the corner. Go through the tunnel and emerge onto PCH for the stunning ocean views you've been waiting for all the way to Malibu.

With several hotels, restaurants, and attractions on PCH, there are many ways to spend hours or days enjoying the beach culture. Ride a Ferris wheel on the Santa Monica Pier, admire art at the Getty Villa, take a dip at Zuma Beach, and watch surfers catch a wave.

START THIS TOUR IN

LONG BEACH
at Second Street and Pacific Coast Highway. Since PCH travels inland and doesn't have ocean views through the South Bay, you may opt for streets closer to the water once you're in Redondo Beach.

LONG BEACH

> **TIP**
>
> At the *Queen Mary*, you can join a themed historical tour, dine in restaurants, sip a drink in the Observation Bar, and even stay overnight in one of the ship's cabins.

Located about 20 miles south of downtown LA, Long Beach is a major port city comprising waterfront areas, beaches, and residential neighborhoods.

Long Beach was incorporated in 1897. With long stretches of sandy waterfront, Long Beach became a coastal resort town. The Port of Long Beach, founded in 1911, further shaped the city's growth. But while Long Beach has a boatload of attractions and historic sites, its pride and joy is the iconic *Queen Mary*. When the ship made her maiden voyage in 1936, she was considered the grandest ocean liner in history. She's been permanently docked in Long Beach since 1967 and is open to the public for tours, dining, and lodging.

Long Beach also has a history in aerospace. Before the Long Beach Airport was dedicated in 1924, the city's beaches served as a landing strip for biplanes. During the Golden Age of Aviation (about 1918 to 1938), Long Beach attracted many aspiring aviators, including Amelia Earhart, who decided to become a pilot in 1920.

Other historic attractions include Rancho Los Alamitos, a restored 20th-century working ranch and city landmark twice listed on the National Register of Historic Places. Historic districts include the Wrigley area (named after chewing gum magnate William Wrigley Jr.) and Bluff Park.

Visit!

AQUARIUM OF THE PACIFIC
100 Aquarium Way
562-590-3100

SHORELINE VILLAGE
429 Shoreline Village Dr.
562-435-2668

MUSEUM OF LATIN AMERICAN ART
On the campus of California State University, Long Beach.
628 Alamitos Ave.
562-437-1689

Eat!

JOE JOST'S (1924)
(cash only)
2803 E Anaheim St.
562-439-5446

Stay!

QUEEN MARY
1126 Queens Hwy.
562-435-3510

> **FUN FACT:**
> The Port of Long Beach is the second-busiest container port in the US. It's located adjacent to the Port of Los Angeles.

Commodore Everette Hoard has been fascinated with the *Queen Mary* since childhood. He's worked on the ship for over 40 years.

to Do!

CATALINA ISLAND
Catalina Express operates boats between San Pedro, Long Beach and Dana Point, and Catalina Island.
320 Golden Shore
Berth 95

GONDOLA GETAWAY
5437 E Ocean Blvd.
562-433-9595

RANCHO LOS ALAMITOS
6400 E Bixby Hill Rd.
526-431-3541

SHORELINE PEDESTRIAN BIKE PATH
Also known as the Long Beach Bike Path, a 4.5-mile path from Shoreline Village to Belmont Shore.

DIRECTIONS TO WILMINGTON: Follow Pacific Coast Highway/CA-1. It travels through the Los Alamitos Traffic Circle (roundabout) at Lakewood Boulevard and PCH.

DIRECTIONS TO ADJACENT SAN PEDRO: Not on PCH but nearby and worth a visit. If you go to San Pedro, take West Twenty-Fifth Street as Palos Verdes Drive South ends. Head north on South Pacific Avenue toward one of San Pedro's distinctive landmarks, Vincent Thomas Bridge.

DETOUR— SAN PEDRO

While PCH doesn't pass directly through San Pedro, it's nearby, and it's worth visiting this waterfront town for its rich maritime history. In its early days, it was a trading post for Spanish missionary monks from Mission San Gabriel Arcángel who depended on supplies from Spain. In 1805, the *Lelia Byrd* was the first American trading ship to call at San Pedro.

Thanks to Phineas Banning, a young entrepreneur from Delaware, the Point Fermin Lighthouse was built in 1874 as the first navigational light into San Pedro Bay, which became part of the Port of Los Angeles—also known as the Los Angeles World Cruise Center.

Eat!

22ND ST LANDING SEAFOOD GRILL & BAR
141 W 22nd St.
310-548-4400

GREEN ONION MEXICAN RESTAURANT
145 W 6th St.
310-519-0631

SAN PEDRO FISH MARKET AND RESTAURANT
706 S Harbor Blvd.
310-832-4251

THE CORNER STORE
1118 W 37th St.
310-832-2424

The Vincent Thomas Bridge is a 1,500-foot-long suspension bridge, crossing Los Angeles Harbor. It's the only suspension bridge in the Greater Los Angeles area.

The port was founded on December 9, 1907, and is one of the busiest ports in the US. Since 1913, the Angels Gate Lighthouse has welcomed vessels to the port with an emerald-green beacon. (Point Fermin ceased operation during WWII.)

Even if you're not cruising, there's a lot to do on the LA Waterfront, which has experienced major development over the years.

The waterfront is home to many attractions, including the Battleship USS *Iowa* Museum, SS *Lane Victory*, Los Angeles Maritime Museum (housed in the historic Municipal Ferry Terminal building), restaurants, a fish market, and more.

San Pedro is a mix of industrial, commercial, and residential areas with historic homes. The San Pedro Bay Historical Society places plaques on the exterior walls of homes designated as historic Craftsman-style architecture.

Visit!

FORT MACARTHUR MUSEUM
3601 S Gaffey St.
310-241-0846

KOREAN BELL OF FRIENDSHIP IN ANGELS GATE PARK
The cast bronze bell was a gift to the US by the South Korean government in 1976.
3601 S Gaffey St.
310-548-7705

POINT FERMIN LIGHTHOUSE (1874)
(free admission)
807 W Paseo Del Mar
310-241-0684

POINT FERMIN PARK
807 W Paseo Del Mar

to Do!

CABRILLO MARINE AQUARIUM
(formerly Cabrillo Marine Museum)
3720 Stephen M. White Dr.
310-548-7562

LOS ANGELES MARITIME MUSEUM
Berth 84, Foot of Sixth St.
310-548-7618

WARNER GRAND THEATRE
The theater opened in 1913 and hosts films, concerts, and youth performances.
478 W 6th St.
310-548-2493

TAKE THE HARBOR FREEWAY (110-N). Drive three miles and exit at Pacific Coast Highway/CA-1

WILMINGTON

A young Phineas Banning put Wilmington on the map in the late 1850s. Banning, who named the town after his birthplace in Delaware, is credited with helping to establish the Port of Los Angeles in neighboring San Pedro. For his role, he was named the "Father of the Port of Los Angeles."

He was an ambitious young man who operated a freighting business and stagecoach line between Wilmington and San Pedro. And during the Civil War, he ceded land to the Union Army to build the Drum Barracks. It's the last remaining American Civil War–era military building in the LA area and is open to the public as the Drum Barracks Civil War Museum.

Banning also built a 23-room home for his family in Wilmington in 1864. The design is Greek Revival, and it is open to the public as a living museum.

When the Don Hotel opened in the summer of 1929, it was considered the most elaborate hotel in the harbor district. It catered to tourists traveling to and from Santa Catalina Island.

In the 1930s, many prominent guests stayed at the hotel, including publishing magnate William Randolph Hearst and singer Bing Crosby. However, by the 1980s, the clientele had changed from the prestigious to the homeless, who stayed there under an LA County welfare voucher program. In 1999, the hotel converted to the Don Senior Apartments.

Today, Wilmington is the third-largest oil field in the US and is known for its heavy concentration of industry.

Eat!

CHOWDER BARGE
611 N Henry Ford Ave.
(E Anaheim St.)
310-830-7937

ISSAC'S CAFÉ
632 N Fries Ave.
310-830-4933

TAQUERIA EL TACO LOCO #4
128 E Pacific Coast Hwy.
310-513-1313

Visit!

BANNING MUSEUM
401 E M St.
310-548-7777

DRUM BARRACKS CIVIL WAR MUSEUM
1052 N Banning Blvd.
310-548-7509

STAY ON Pacific Coast Highway to Torrance.

TORRANCE

Torrance is a coastal city with a 1.5-mile beachfront, but it's also home to the Madrona Marsh, a seasonal wetlands area.

Until 1912, Torrance was part of a Spanish land grant owned by the Dominguez family and was mostly unpopulated. In 1912, real estate developer Jared Sidney Torrance purchased 2,800 acres to create a modern industrial city. The city was developed by famous landscape architects Olmsted and Olmsted; building architect Irving J. Gill; and Frank Lloyd Wright Jr., who helped design landscaping.

Incorporated as a city in 1921, Torrance evolved through gradual annexation to 21 square miles. In the late 1940s, Torrance experienced a housing boom, boosting the city's population and development of businesses, shopping centers, and cultural attractions.

Torrance Beach, which has views of the Palos Verdes Peninsula, has nice amenities that include lifeguards, a beach café, outdoor showers, and restrooms.

Torrance is also the starting point for the Strand, a popular coastal bike path that travels to Santa Monica.

Since about 2009, Torrance has had a growing craft beer scene. Visit one of the local breweries, such as Monkish Brewing Co. or Smog City Brewing Co., to sample some unique and flavorful brews.

Eat!

COZZI CAFÉ
1413 Marcelina Ave.
424-558-8050

GIULIANO'S DELICATESSEN & BAKERY
3849 Torrance Blvd.
310-540-2500

HOPSAINT BREWING COMPANY
5160 W 190th St.
310-214-4677

KING'S HAWAIIAN BAKERY & RESTAURANT
2808 W Sepulveda Blvd.
310-530-0050

RED CAR BREWERY & RESTAURANT
1266 Sartori Ave.
310-782-0222

THE LOCAL PLACE BAKERY & CAFÉ
18605 S Western Ave.
310-523-3233

Visit!

CHEN ART GALLERY
Call to schedule a tour.
1625 Abalone Ave.
310-222-9192

LA ROMERIA PARK
19501 Inglewood Ave.
310-618-2930

TORRANCE CULTURAL ARTS CENTER
3330 Civic Center Dr.
310-781-7150

TORRANCE HISTORICAL SOCIETY
1345 Post Ave.
310-328-5392

WILSON PARK
2200 Crenshaw Blvd.
310-972-7760

TIP

Visit the Torrance Historical Society & Museum, housed in the city's first Main Library, which was built in 1936. The Torrance Historical Society also hosts walking tours of Old Torrance.

to Do!

MADRONA MARSH PRESERVE AND NATURE CENTER
3201 Plaza Del Amo
310-782-3989

TORRANCE CERTIFIED FARMERS' MARKET
(Tuesdays and Saturdays)
Charles H. Wilson Park
2200 Crenshaw Blvd.
310-781-7520

STAY ON Pacific Coast Highway (Highway 1) to Redondo Beach.

REDONDO BEACH

Redondo Beach is a quintessential California surf town. After all, it's here that surfing got its start in California. Oahu native George Freeth introduced the Polynesian art of surfing to Californians in the early 1900s. It created a laid-back surf culture that has since defined Redondo ("round" in Spanish).

Redondo was incorporated in 1892 and was an early port of Los Angeles. Redondo's short-lived salt plant in the mid-1800s gave way to the lumber and shipping industries that contributed to the city's growth and reputation as a resort town. But with the opening of the Port of Los Angeles in San Pedro, Redondo lost its shipping trade. Following slow growth during the Great Depression, Redondo rebounded in the 1950s and 1960s.

The unique horseshoe-shaped pier was built in 1888 but was destroyed several times due to storms, and a fire in 1988. It was rebuilt (completed in 1995), and the new 70,000-square-foot pier is a lively place with about 50 eateries and shops. Popular places include Tony's on the Pier (known as Old Tony's and the place for tasty mai tais). The family-owned restaurant and bar was established in 1952 by a commercial fisherman.

Redondo Beach Pier

Meanwhile, after 53 years of planning, King Harbor was finally dedicated in 1966 and currently consists of four marinas, three yacht clubs, hotels, fish markets, waterfront restaurants, and ocean-view apartments and offices. It's the hub for kayaking, standup paddle boarding, sailing, and whale-watching excursions. There's also a heated seaside lagoon.

TIP

Visit Heritage Court to see two historic beach cottages: the 1906 Morrell House, and the 1904 Queen Anne House, which serves as the City's Historical Museum.

Eat!

BALEENKITCHEN
260 Portofino Way
310-372-1202

CAPTAIN KIDD'S FISH MARKET & RESTAURANT
209 N Harbor Dr.
310-372-7703

QUALITY SEAFOOD
Family-owned fish market and restaurant since 1953.
130 S International Boardwalk
310-372-6408

R/10 SOCIAL HOUSE
179 N Harbor Dr.
310-798-2500

RIVIERA MEXICAN CANTINA
207 N Harbor Dr.
310-374-2689

SEA LEVEL AT THE SHADE HOTEL
655 N Harbor Dr.
310-921-8950

Visit!

HERITAGE COURT
302 Flagler Ln.

HOPKINS WILDERNESS PARK
1102 Camino Real
310-318-0670

KING HARBOR
200 Portofino Way
310-318-0681

REDONDO BEACH PIER
Fisherman's Wharf

Stay!

CRYSTAL COVE APARTMENTS
211 S Yacht Club Way
310-376-0421

PORTOFINO HOTEL & MARINA
(part of Noble House Hotels & Resorts)
260 Portofino Way
310-372-1202

REDONDO BEACH HOTEL
400 N Harbor Dr.
310-376-0746

SHADE HOTEL
655 N Harbor Dr.
310-921-8940

to Do!

REDONDO BEACH PERFORMING ARTS CENTER
1935 Manhattan Beach Blvd.
310-937-6607

DRIVE ALONG PACIFIC COAST HIGHWAY. To reach the Hermosa Pier, turn left on 1 Pier Avenue.

HERMOSA BEACH

It's understandable how Hermosa got its name, which means "beautiful" in Spanish. It is indeed that, but the laid-back beach vibe, historic pier, and Strand boardwalk enhance its appeal.

Just over one square mile in size, Hermosa is home to about 19,000 residents. It's a small town steeped in surf culture. At the foot of the pier is a statue of Tim Kelly, who was a Los Angeles County lifeguard, surfer, and youth worker admired by young South Bay surfers.

The two-mile Strand boardwalk was built in 1901, underwent restoration, and was finally completed in 1926. The first pier, constructed in 1904, was built of wood, and it was rebuilt after part of it washed away in 1913. The next (and current) pier was rebuilt with concrete and asphalt and juts 1,000 feet into the water.

The city's extensive beautification projects over the last 15-plus years have included the renovation of pedestrian-friendly Pier Plaza in 1997. With comfortable places to dine and relax, it's a nice addition to the pier and the Strand.

Even as the city evolves with new restaurants and shops, many historic places still stand. Mickey's Italian Delicatessen opened in 1953 and became a favorite pizza joint with locals.

Hermosa Beach is a vibrant beach town with live music, festivals, special events, and summer concerts.

The surf statue is dedicated to the memory of Tim Kelly.

The Strand

Eat!

BROTHER'S BURRITOS
24 11th St.
310-372-0707

GOOD STUFF
(also in Redondo, El Segundo, and Palos Verdes)
1286 The Strand
310-374-2334

LIGHTHOUSE CAFÉ
A jazz club since 1949, the venue serves bar food and has live music.
30 Pier Ave.
310-376-9833

MARTHA'S
25 22nd St. (between Hermosa Ave. and the Strand)
310-376-7786

MICKEY'S ITALIAN DELI
101 Hermosa Ave.
310-376-2330

ROSA'S RESTAURANT
322 Pacific Coast Hwy.
310-374-9094

TOWER 12
53 Pier Ave.
310-379-6400

Visit!

HERMOSA BEACH MUSEUM
The small museum is located on the right side and toward the back of the Hermosa Community Center.
710 Pier Ave.
310-318-9421

to Do!

HERMOSA BEACH PIER AND PLAZA
1 Pier Ave.

PACIFIC COAST HIGHWAY becomes Sepulveda Boulevard in Manhattan Beach.

MANHATTAN BEACH

Manhattan Beach is among the three Beach Cities (along with Redondo and Hermosa), but many consider it Beverly Hills by the beach. From its inception, Manhattan Beach seemed destined to be an upscale community. It was first known as Shore Acres and then Potencia until brothers John and Stewart Merrill bought and renamed the city Manhattan Beach, after an upscale beach resort on Coney Island in New York.

Roundhouse Aquarium on Manhattan Beach Pier

The Manhattan Beach Pier was built around 1896 as an energy source (by capturing ocean waves generating energy) for the future beach community. Two storms, one in 1897 and another in 1913, destroyed the pier. The third pier was built in 1920 and remains standing. The Roundhouse Aquarium at the end of the pier was added in 1922.

One year after Manhattan Beach was incorporated in 1912, developer George Peck bought the north end of the area and began recruiting people to buy homes by the ocean. The area was a mound of sand dunes until the Kuhn Brothers Construction Company leveled the sites in the 1920s and 1930s.

The sand was sold and shipped to Waikiki, Hawaii, to transform its reef and rocky beach into a sandy beach. Over the next 10 years, sand from Manhattan Beach was loaded onto Santa Fe Railroad cars, transferred to ships or barges in San Pedro Harbor, and transported to Honolulu.

Later, after WWII, Manhattan Beach became a desirable beach town.

Eat!

THE KETTLE
1138 Highland Ave.
310-545-8511

THE TAVERN ON MAIN
123 Main St.
310-322-3645

UNCLE BILL'S PANCAKE HOUSE
1305 Highland Ave.
310-545-5177

Visit!

MANHATTAN BEACH HISTORICAL SOCIETY
1601 Manhattan Beach Blvd.
310-374-7575

to Do!

MANHATTAN BEACH CERTIFIED FARMERS' MARKET
Every Tuesday (11 a.m. to 3 p.m.)
Downtown Manhattan Beach

ROUNDHOUSE AQUARIUM
Manhattan Beach Pier
310-379-8117

STAY ON Sepulveda Boulevard, which becomes PCH/CA-1 in El Segundo.

EL SEGUNDO

El Segundo is a beachside city home to oil and aerospace industries, residential neighborhoods, and a historic downtown area.

El Segundo got its name (meaning "second" in Spanish) because it was the second Standard Oil refinery on the West Coast. The first one was in Richmond, in Northern California. In 1911, the oil refinery purchased land in what would become El Segundo. The refinery, renamed Chevron in 1984, is the city's largest employer.

At one time, the industrial wharves servicing oil tanker ships crowded the waterfront area, creating sewage and pollution along the narrow beach. But the expansion of the Hyperion wastewater treatment plant in the 1980s, along with the removal of piers and an underwater oil terminal built a few miles offshore, helped clean up the area.

Eat!

ALI'I FISH COMPANY
(Hawaiian)
409 E Grand Ave.
310-616-3484

SLICE & PINT
130 W Grand Ave.
310-648-8479

RICHMOND BAR & GRILL
145 Richmond St.
310-322-7397

THE TAVERN ON MAIN
123 Main St.
310-322-3645

Visit!

OLD TOWN MUSIC HALL
140 Richmond St.
310-322-2592

Old Town Music Hall houses the 1925 Mighty Wurlitzer theater pipe organ, consisting of over 2,600 pipes.

Dredged sand was used to restore and enlarge El Segundo Beach. Although the beach still faces the oil refinery and tall smokestacks, high fences and walls help block some of the views. The beach has a paved bike path.

While in town, visit Old Town Music Hall, home to the Mighty Wurlitzer theater organ. The hometown theater opened as the El Segundo State Theater in 1921. After debuting as Old Town Music Hall in the 1960s, it began presenting Hollywood Golden Age films, as well as silent films accompanied live on the pipe organ. The two chandeliers were bought for $25 each from a junkyard in 1968.

TO TAKE A COASTAL ROUTE to visit Playa del Rey, take Imperial Highway to Vista del Mar. This road travels by Dockweiler State Beach.

STAY ON PCH and follow signs for Highway 1 North. Go through the Sepulveda Boulevard Tunnel (under two airport runways) that leads to Lincoln Boulevard/CA-1. You'll be under the flight path of the Los Angeles International Airport.

AFTER THE TUNNEL, STAY ON LINCOLN BLVD/CA-1. There's a sign (to your left) for Playa del Rey. The road travels through the neighborhoods of Playa Vista and Westchester.

PLAYA DEL REY

Home to about 16,000 people, Playa del Rey (Spanish for "beach of the king") is a small coastal community adjacent to centuries-old wetlands.

Aviation was part of its early history. In 1910, the Wright brothers established the Wright Company, which served as a production facility for their aircrafts and their test flights.

At the beginning of the 20th century, the Pacific Electric Red Car transit system and automobiles brought more people and development to the area.

Playa Del Rey evolved with residential neighborhoods in the 20th and 21st centuries.

For centuries, the Ballona Wetlands encompassed 2,000 acres. But development, including the creation of the Marina Del Rey Harbor, cut into a chunk of that, causing concern among locals. In 2003, the Friends of Ballona Wetlands, along with the State of California and the developer of Playa Del Rey, agreed to preserve about 600 acres of the wetlands.

The seaside community's beach and parks are inviting for outdoor activities and picnics. Playa Del Rey Beach is operated by Los Angeles County and has volleyball courts and a paved bike path called the Marvin Braude Bike Trail. A grass park across the street is home to Del Rey Lagoon.

TIP

Learn about the history of Playa del Rey and the neighboring communities of Westchester and Playa Vista at the Westchester/Playa Historical Society Discovery Center, 6207 W 87th Street, Westchester. wphistoricalsociety.org

Courtesy of Friends of Ballona Wetlands.

Visit!

BALLONA DISCOVERY PARK
13110 Bluff Creek Dr.
310-306-5994

BALLONA WETLANDS
303 Culver Blvd.

DEL REY LAGOON
6660 Esplanade Pl.
310-836-1040

PLAYA DEL REY BEACH
Culver Blvd. and Pacific Ave.

TITMOUSE PARK
415 Culver Blvd.

VISTA DEL MAR PARK
Vista Del Mar and Century Blvd.
310-836-1040

Eat!

THE SHACK
185 Culver Blvd.
310-823-6222

TO REACH MARINA DEL REY from PCH/CA-1, turn left on Fiji Way.

OR, FROM PLAYA DEL REY to the marina: Take Vista del Mar to Culver Boulevard, keep right on West Jefferson Boulevard, turn left on Lincoln Boulevard, turn left on Bali Way, turn right on Admiralty Way.

The Warehouse Restaurant

MARINA DEL REY

Compared to many other communities in the LA Basin, Marina del Rey is young—just 60 years old. The harbor was dedicated on April 10, 1965. But the land and water on which it's built have a long history.

With its proximity to the ocean and a salt marsh fed by fresh water from Ballona Creek, the land now occupied by Marina del Rey has served many purposes. Thousands of years ago, the Tonga People settled in the area and harvested seeds, hunted, and fished. The Spanish arrived in 1542, and later Europeans used the land for duck hunting and fishing.

But it was developer Moye C. Wicks who envisioned a commercial harbor for the city of LA in 1887. The plan was to develop the estuary and wetland of neighboring Playa del Rey into a commercial port. But without proper equipment, the salt marsh kept filling in. The harbor was eventually built in Long Beach, and plans changed for Marina del Rey, which was developed from the mid-1950s to 1963. The first hotel was the Marina del Rey Hotel in 1964.

The first two buildings were the Warehouse restaurant (still there) and Pieces of Eight, renamed Whiskey Red's. Both are in Fisherman's Village, which was built in 1967 and is a lively area with restaurants, shops, and

Eat!

BRIZO BAR & RESTAURANT
4360 Via Marina
424-443-5807

KILLER CAFÉ
4213 Admiralty Way
310-578-2250

LIGHTHOUSE FOUNTAIN & GRILL
13735 Fiji Way

PIZZARITO
4371 Glencoe Ave.
310-823-7333

SALT RESTAURANT & BAR
13534 Bali Way
424-289-8223

THE WAREHOUSE RESTAURANT
4499 Admiralty Way
310-823-5451

TONY P'S DOCKSIDE GRILL
4445 Admiralty Way
310-823-4534

WHISKEY RED'S
13813 Fiji Way
310-823-4522

Visit!

FISHERMAN'S VILLAGE
13755 Fiji Way

MARINA DEL REY HISTORICAL SOCIETY
13737 Fiji Way #C3
424-391-6976

TIP

Park in Fisherman's Village to explore the marina.

a pretty marina. The Marina del Rey Historical Society is also on the waterfront and houses photos, maps, and other historical items.

Marina del Rey has 10,000 residents, hosts 5,000 vessels, and has miles of public waterfront access.

FROM MARINA DEL REY TO VENICE: Turn left on Washington Boulevard, and right on Pacific Avenue.

OR, TO BYPASS PLAYA DEL REY and Marina del Rey, and go straight to Venice, stay on Lincoln Boulevard and watch for the Venice sign.

Lighthouse Fountain & Grill in Fisherman's Village

VENICE

This beach town was created by Abbott Kinney in 1905 as part of his Venice of America plan to re-create the appearance and ambiance of Venice, Italy. He built canals, waterways, pedestrian bridges, a lagoon, and a commercial district.

Only six canals remain from the elaborate network he created, and they are located in the Venice Canal Historic District. Multimillion-dollar homes, some with private docks, and non motorized watercraft line the pretty canals, located a few blocks from Venice Beach.

But it's the sunny, wide beach; pier; and funky boardwalk that Venice is best known for. Mimes, musicians, jugglers, and other street performers can be seen along the famous boardwalk, which is flanked by cafés, shops, and Small World Books (established in 1969). There's a waterfront skatepark, the iconic outdoor Muscle Beach Gym, and sports courts. Popular activities include renting beach cruisers to peddle along the 22-mile paved Marvin Braude Bike Trail. Take a walk along the 1,300-foot-long Venice Pier, built in 1963.

Venice not only has a classic beach culture but also a trendy shopping area along Abbott Kinney Boulevard, a lively, one-mile-long street with restaurants, coffee bars, stylish boutiques, and galleries from Washington Boulevard to Main Street.

Venice has an array of restaurants and bars. Hinano Café, around since 1962, states on its website that it was Jim Morrison's favorite Venice hangout.

Venice boardwalk shops

Eat!

CASABLANCA
220 Lincoln Blvd.
310-392-5751

HINANO CAFÉ
15 Washington Blvd.
310-822-3902

LA CABAÑA
738 Rose Ave.
310-392-7973

QUIADAIYN RESTAURANT
12326 Venice Blvd.
310-313-7654

THE ROSE VENICE
220 Rose Ave.
310-399-0711

Stay!

HOTEL ERWIN
1697 Pacific Ave.
310-452-1111

VENICE V HOTEL
5 Westminster Ave.
310-912-6488

THE KINNEY HOTEL
737 Washington Blvd.
310-821-4455

Visit!

SMALL WORLD BOOKS
1407 Ocean Front Walk
310-399-2360

to Do!

FIRST FRIDAYS, on the first Friday of each month, feature live music and food trucks, 5:00 p.m. to 9:30 p.m.

TIP

Park the car and stroll along the walkways of Venice Canals, located off Twenty-Fifth Street in Venice.

FROM VENICE TO SANTA MONICA:
Follow Lincoln Boulevard

SANTA MONICA

While the Santa Monica Pier is the top tourist attraction, there are many things to enjoy in this iconic SoCal beach city, which dates to 1875.

After its founding, the first lots sold for $75 and $500. Soon, houses and stores were built, a general store opened, and a newspaper was published. Santa Monica was incorporated in November 1886, and by 1905, the population was 7,208. Santa Monica became a resort town after the establishment of the Arcadia Hotel, located on Ocean Avenue from 1886 to 1909.

Santa Monica drew the attention of famous carousel manufacturer Charles I. D. Looff, who built his beachside Looff Hippodrome and Pleasure Pier amusement park in 1916. He built his pier next to the Santa Monica Pier, which served as a conduit for the city's sewage.

The side-by-side piers comprise the bustling Santa Monica Pier, which anchors restaurants, shops, vendor carts, and the Pacific Park amusement park. There are several rides, but the most thrilling is the solar-powered Pacific Wheel (Ferris wheel), looming nine stories high above the waves.

Santa Monica is also famous for its 3.5 miles of wide, sandy beaches—the perfect place to claim a spot and enjoy the surf and warm sunshine.

Beyond the beach, Santa Monica has several farmers markets and shopping areas. The pedestrian-only Third Street Promenade and adjacent Santa Monica Place are outdoor shopping areas with various events.

Marion Davies guest house at Annenberg Community Beach House.

The Looff Hippodrome on the Santa Monica Pier was the last work of carousel manufacturer Charles I. D. Looff.

Eat!

BIG DEAN'S OCEAN FRONT CAFÉ
1615 Ocean Front Walk
310-393-2666

CHEZ JAY
1657 Ocean Ave.
310-395-1741

HOT DOG ON A STICK
(near Muscle Beach)
1633 Ocean Front Walk
310-395-4673

THE GALLEY
2442 Main St.
310-452-1934

THE LOBSTER
1602 Ocean Ave.
310-458-9294

RAE'S
2901 Pico Blvd.
424-272-9016

THE MISFIT BAR & RESTAURANT
225 Santa Monica Blvd.
310-656-9800

Visit!

ANNENBERG COMMUNITY BEACH HOUSE
415 Pacific Coast Hwy.
310-458-4904

SANTA MONICA HISTORY MUSEUM
(free the first Sunday of each month)
1350 Seventh St.
310-395-2290

to Do!

SANTA MONICA FARMERS MARKETS
310-458-8712

DOWNTOWN FARMERS MARKET
8 a.m. to 1 p.m.
Wednesdays (frequented by local star chefs) and Saturdays
Arizona Ave. and 2nd St.

MAIN STREET FARMERS MARKET
8:30 a.m. to 1:30 p.m.
Sundays
2640 Main St.

SATURDAY PICO BOULEVARD FARMERS MARKET
8 a.m. to 1 p.m.
2233 Pico Blvd.

SANTA MONICA PIER AND PACIFIC PARK
200 Santa Monica Pier
310-458-8900

TIP

Visit the Annenberg Community Beach House, which has a beachfront café and swimming pool. It's located on the site of a mansion (now demolished) built for Marion Davies by William Randolph Hearst. An on-site guesthouse is open for tours.

415 Pacific Coast Hwy.
310-458-4904

Stay!

HOTEL CASA DEL MAR
1910 Ocean Way
310-581-5533

PALIHOUSE
1001 Third St.
310-394-1279

THE GEORGIAN
1415 Ocean Ave.
310-395-9945

TAKE LINCOLN BOULEVARD to Olympic Boulevard, and turn left at the sign for CA-1 North, which goes through a tunnel and leads to the scenic section of Pacific Coast Highway.

Interior courtyard at the Getty Villa, which opened in 1974.

PACIFIC PALISADES

Attracting fewer tourists than neighboring beach towns, Pacific Palisades is a secluded, mostly residential community of about 27,000.

The scenic coastal town has parks, hiking trails, and three miles of beaches: Will Rogers State Beach, Sunset Point Beach, and Ginger Rogers Beach. It's also home to the Getty Villa Museum, Self-Realization Fellowship Lake Shrine, and Will Rogers State Historic Park.

The land was mostly uninhabited until the community's founding in 1922, by a Methodist organization with plans for a religious commune. Charles H. Scott and the Southern California Methodist Episcopal Church bought the land. Followers bought lots, and by 1925 there were 100 homes.

The Pacific Palisades Historical Society owns and maintains Founders Oak Island, considered the community's birthplace. The secluded area also became a refuge for many Jewish people fleeing pre-war Germany and the Holocaust.

TIP

While the Self-Realization Fellowship Lake Shrine is open daily, the temple is open only on Sundays.

Will Rogers State Historic Park was created in 1944 when his widow, Betty, donated the family ranch and land for Will Rogers State Beach to the State of California. In January 2025, wildfires in Pacific Palisades destroyed Will Rogers's ranch. California State Parks was able to evacuate some of the cultural and historical artifacts, including artwork.

Nearby, the Getty Villa Museum houses Greek and Roman antiquities in a re-created Roman country home with gardens and fountains.

Also in the vicinity, the serene Self-Realization Fellowship Lake Shrine has a walking path that surrounds a large lake and meditation gardens.

Visit!

SELF-REALIZATION FELLOWSHIP LAKE SHRINE
Free, but reservations required.
17190 Sunset Blvd.
310-454-4114

TEMESCAL CANYON PARK
15900 Pacific Coast Hwy.
310-836-1040

WILL ROGERS STATE BEACH
17000 CA-1

WILL ROGERS STATE HISTORIC PARK
1501 Will Rogers State Park Rd.
310-230-2017

The Self-Realization Fellowship Lake Shrine has a natural spring-fed lake, mediation gardens, and the Mahatma Ghandi World Peace Memorial.

to Do!

GETTY VILLA
Free, but timed-entry reservation required.
17985 Pacific Coast Hwy.
310-440-7300

Eat!

PORTA VIA
1063 N Swarthmore Ave.
310-499-2989

FOLLOW PACIFIC COAST HIGHWAY.

MALIBU

While Malibu enjoys celebrity status, it rolls out the welcome mat to everyone. Stretching for more than 21 miles along the coast, Malibu has sunny beaches ideal for surfing and sunbathing, as well as historic sites and attractions.

In California's early days, the beaches were home to Chumash Indians, and shoreline caves served as hideouts for smugglers and pirates. Settlers began arriving in the 1700s, but the development of Malibu as an upscale residential community began in 1928, with an exclusive beach area that served as a hideaway for celebrities. It became known as the Malibu Movie Colony.

Around the same time, Hawaiian surfer Duke Kahanamoku taught the sport to locals. Malibu's south-facing beaches create the perfect curl for surfing.

A popular spot to watch surfers is Surfrider Beach by the Malibu Pier. Malibu's iconic beaches for swimming and soaking up sun include Zuma Beach. In winter, there's a good chance of seeing migrating gray whales from Malibu's north end at Point Dume.

TIP

Visit the historic Adamson House. While the grounds are open daily, guided house tours take place 11 a.m. to 2 p.m. Wednesdays, Thursdays, Fridays, and Saturdays.
310-456-8432

Adamson House

Paradise Cove Beach Café

In addition to sun and surf, Malibu has cultural attractions, such as the 1929 Adamson House and Malibu Lagoon Museum, which represent local history.

Stay!

HOTEL JUNE MALIBU
28920 Pacific Coast Hwy.
424-644-0517

MALIBU BEACH INN
22878 Pacific Coast Hwy.
800-462-5428

SURFRIDER HOTEL
23033 Pacific Coast Hwy.
310-526-6158

to Do!

CONNEMARA RANCH
(horseback riding)
400 Kanan Dume Rd.
619-518-5828

MALIBU PIER
23000 Pacific Coast Hwy.

Visit!

ADAMSON HOUSE AND MALIBU LAGOON MUSEUM
23200 E Pacific Coast Hwy.
310-456-8432

LEO CARRILLO STATE PARK
35000 Pacific Coast Hwy.
310-457-8144

Eat!

GEOFFREY'S MALIBU
27400 Pacific Coast Hwy
310-457-1519

MALIBU COUNTRY MART
John's Garden for sandwiches is among the eateries.
3835 Cross Creek Rd.
310-456-8377

MALIBU SEAFOOD
25653 Pacific Coast Hwy.
310-456-3430

NEPTUNE'S NET
42505 Pacific Coast Hwy.
310-457-3095

PARADISE COVE BEACH CAFÉ
28128 Pacific Coast Hwy.
310-457-2503

Valencia
Canyon County
Santa Clarita
Newhall
Placerita Canyon State Park
SANTA SUSANA MTS.
BIG MOUNTAIN
Oat Mtn. 3,747
Omelveny Park
Sylmar
San Fernando
Pacoima
Hansen L.
SUNLAND
GRANADA HILLS
RONALD REAGAN FRWY
Chatsworth
SAN FERNANDO VALLEY
NORDHOFF
NORTHRIDGE
Simi Valley
SIMI HILLS
Canoga Park
Reseda
Burbank
Oak Park
Ahmanson Ranch
Agoura Hills
Tarzana
Encino
Woodland Hills
Los Encinos State Hist. Park
Encino Reservoir
North Hollywood
Toluca Lake
Studio City
Universal City
Griffith Park
Sherman Oaks
Laurel Canyon
Calabasas
Topanga State Park
Los Angeles
Hollywood
Cornell
Malibu Creek State Park
Mulholland Highway
West Hollywood
Bel Air
SANTA MONICA MOUNTAINS NATL. REC. AREA
Topanga
Will Rogers State Historic Park
Beverly Hills
SANTA MONICA MTS.
Pacific Palisades
Malibu
Will Rogers State Beach
Santa Monica State Beach
Santa Monica
Culver City
View Park
Windsor Hills
Venice
Marina del Rey
Ladera Hts.
WESTCHESTER
Inglewood
Santa Monica Bay
Playa del Rey
Lennox
Athens
El Segundo
Manhattan Beach
Lawndale
Hermosa Beach
Redondo Beach
Torrance
Palos Verdes Estates
Lomita
PACIFIC OCEAN
Palos Verdes Point
Rolling Hills
Rancho Palos Verdes
Point Vicente
SAN PEDRO

SANTA MONICA MOUNTAINS

Several canyon roads snake through the beautiful Santa Monica Mountains, which span from the Hollywood Hills to Ventura. The scenic canyon roads connect the San Fernando and Conejo valleys to the Pacific Ocean and beach towns.

Whether you start your drive from Pacific Coast Highway or the valleys, the roadways are picturesque and provide many rest stops. Some, like Topanga Canyon and Laurel Canyon, are residential, while others are rural, with winding two-lane highways offering sweeping views.

Mulholland Highway and Mulholland Drive are named after civil engineer William Mulholland. The 24-mile Mulholland Drive travels from the Cahuenga Pass through the Hollywood Hills along the ridgeline, offering panoramic views of the San Fernando Valley, Los Angeles, and iconic landmarks, which include the Hollywood Bowl, Hollywood Sign, and Griffith Park Observatory. The drive begins at the intersection of Cahuenga Boulevard and the 101 Freeway in Hollywood.

Mulholland Highway, a scenic route with historic sites, travels between the 101 Freeway at Las Virgenes/Malibu Canyon and PCH near Malibu at Leo Carrillo State Park. If you're starting from the valley, Calabasas is your gateway city.

The woodsy Topanga Canyon, which connects Malibu with the western San Fernando Valley, is the main roadway for Topanga residents.

START THIS TOUR IN

TOPANGA CANYON; from US 101 North, exit at Topanga Canyon Boulevard, drive south.

Artistic director Ellen Geer (Will Geer's daughter) is among the family members who work in various roles at the Will Geer Theatricum Botanicum open-air theater.

TOPANGA CANYON

Driving through Topanga Canyon, it's easy to understand why the Tonga People considered this a sacred place. The vistas and the shifting light through whispering oak trees create a mystical feeling.

The 20-mile road carves through this eclectic mountain community, home to whimsical boutiques, cozy eateries tucked in the woods, road vendors, and art installations. It's one of LA's most unique and enchanting communities.

For decades, the area attracted artists and musicians for inspiration, and was home to many of them, including Woody Gutherie and Neil Young (who recorded *After the Gold Rush* in the basement of his Topanga home).

When Will Geer, grandpa on *The Waltons*, was blacklisted by Hollywood, he and his wife, actress Herta Ware, moved their family to the canyon, where they sold vegetables and fruits from their garden and debuted the Will Geer Theatricum Botanicum in 1973.

After his death in 1978 (he's buried on-site), the family and a small troupe of actors transformed Theatricum into a professional repertory theater company recognized internationally for its interpretation of Shakespeare's works. In addition to live productions, the family-owned-and-operated company offers a variety of workshops for all ages.

Eat!

CAFÉ MIMOSA
395 S Topanga Canyon Blvd.
310-455-4341

CAFÉ ON 27
1861 N Topanga Canyon Blvd.
424-272-7267

INN OF THE SEVENTH RAY
128 Old Topanga Canyon Rd.
310-455-1311

Visit!

HIDDEN TREASURES
154 S Topanga Canyon Blvd.
310-455-2998

SPIRAL STAIRCASE
128 Old Topanga Canyon Rd.
310-455-3370

to Do!

TOPANGA STATE PARK
20828 Entrada Rd.
310-455-2465

WILL GEER THEATRICUM BOTANICUM
1419 N Topanga Canyon Blvd.
310-455-3723

Established in 1973, the Inn of the Seventh Ray is nestled in the woods.

MULHOLLAND HIGHWAY
FROM CALABASAS

The Calabasas area has always been a place of refuge—first for the Chumash, next for Spanish settlers, and then for Hollywood celebrities seeking space and privacy.

Until the completion of the 101 Freeway in the late 1960s, Calabasas was a sleepy town. Calabasas Road was the main thoroughfare. But the 101 brought substantial growth, with new homes, businesses, and commercial development like the Commons at Calabasas, a shopping, dining, and entertainment center.

The 25-room Gillette mansion was built for the founder of the Gillette Safety Razor Company.

Still, historic structures abound. The Leonis Adobe Museum and the Plummer House are in Old Town Calabasas. The latter was once the oldest home in West Hollywood. It was moved adjacent to the Leonis property in 1983. Both homes are restored and open to the public.

Next door, the iconic Sagebrush Cantina restaurant is on the land of former stores from the 1920s. The parking lot was once the local jail. Outside was the hanging tree—still there—and it's the identifying logo of the Chamber of Commerce.

Another historic landmark is the Calabasas Schoolhouse bell. It once hung in the original one-room Calabasas School in 1890.

Located at the Gillette Ranch, the Anthony C. Beilenson Interagency Visitor Center features exhibits and interactive displays about the Santa Monica Mountains.

Ready for your Mulholland Highway tour? Begin at the Anthony C. Beilenson Interagency Visitor Center (also the Santa Monica Mountains Interagency Visitor Center), which has many informative exhibits. There are also nearby hiking trails and a picnic area.

The Visitor Center is in a building that was originally a stable built in 1928. Architect Wallace Neff designed the stable, the Spanish Colonial Revival–style mansion, and other structures for King C. Gillette, the inventor of the first disposable razor blade.

Eat!

SAGEBRUSH CANTINA
23527 Calabasas Rd.
818-222-6062

Visit!

ANTHONY C. BEILENSON INTERAGENCY VISITOR CENTER
(at King Gillette Ranch)
26876 Mulholland Hwy.
818-878-0866; 805-370-2301

KING GILLETTE RANCH
26800 Mulholland Hwy.
818-878-0866; 805-370-2301

CALABASAS SCHOOLHOUSE BELL
4029 Las Virgenes Rd.

LEONIS ADOBE MUSEUM
23537 Calabasas Rd.
818-222-6511

PLUMMER HOUSE
23537 Calabasas Rd.

TO START THE MULHOLLAND HIGHWAY TOUR FROM CALABASAS, head south on Las Virgenes Road for three miles, and then turn left onto Mulholland Highway.

CORNELL

Cornell is a pocket neighborhood along Mulholland Highway. At one time it was autonomous but is now considered part of Agoura. Surrounded by parkland and vistas, the Cornell neighborhood begins at the members-only Malibu Lake (a pretty lake visible from the road).

Along the highway are homes, horse properties, and ranches. Among them is Paramount Ranch, which Paramount Pictures leased in 1927 for TV and film productions that included *Dr. Quinn, Medicine Woman*, *Westworld*, and *American Sniper*.

In 2018, the Woolsey Fire destroyed much of Western Town. However, the train depot and chapel remain. The ranch is open to the public to explore the property and to hike on several easy-to-moderate trails.

TIP

Stop by the Rock Store, a casual, popular eatery and hangout for motorcyclists and celebrities. Established by Ed and Veronica Savko in 1961, the building is made of volcanic rock and was a stagecoach stop in the 1910s.

rock-store.com

The chapel used in HBO's *Westworld* survived the 2018 Woolsey Fire at Paramount Ranch.

Eat!

OLD PLACE RESTAURANT
29983 Mulholland Hwy.
818-706-9001

ROCK STORE
30354 Mulholland Hwy.
818-889-1311

Visit!

CORNELL WINE CO.
(adjacent to Old Place restaurant)
29975 Mulholland Hwy.
818-575-7010

PARAMOUNT RANCH
2903 Cornell Rd.
805-370-2301

PETER STRAUSS RANCH
30000 Mulholland Hwy.
805-370-2301

Cornell is also home to iconic establishments, such as the Old Place restaurant, Cornell Wine Co., and the Rock Store restaurant.

A post office that operated from 1884 to 1904 was later turned into the Old Place restaurant, frequented by celebrities such as Steve McQueen and Ali MacGraw in the late 1960s.

AGOURA HILLS

Agoura Hills is an affluent city in the Santa Monica Mountains region. From LA, it's accessible via the 101 Freeway.

Agoura Hills is listed here because, while the city's boundaries don't extend as far as historic Paramount Ranch and the Peter Strauss Ranch along Mulholland Highway, these places have the same zip code.

LAUREL CANYON

Laurel Canyon is a mountainous neighborhood in the Hollywood Hills, bordered by West Hollywood to the west and south, Hollywood to the east, and Studio City to the north.

Until the 20th century, the only way through the rugged canyon was on foot or by mule. In around 1907, a paved road was built in phases, connecting Hollywood and Studio City in the San Fernando Valley.

In the early 20th century, homes were built along the hillside of neighboring Lookout Mountain, forming the heart of the Laurel Canyon neighborhood. The area's proximity to Hollywood attracted writers, artists, and other creative professionals, and it evolved into a rock and roll neighborhood for musicians in the 1960s and 1970s. Frank Zappa (whose former home is known as the Log Cabin), Joni Mitchell, Jim Morrison, Neil Young, James Taylor, and Brian Wilson were among the many musicians who lived in the hills.

Morrison lived in a house near the Canyon Country Store, a small grocery and deli founded in 1913 that often served as an impromptu stage for area musicians. Today the place stands as a shrine, with photos of The Doors, David Crosby, Graham Nash, Joni Mitchell, and other music legends.

Agoura Hills has easy access to these places via Kanan Dume Road, which connects with Mulholland Highway.

If you choose to visit Agoura Hills, it has noteworthy history, too. The area's first home, Reyes Adobe, was built around 1850 and is situated in a residential area. At the Reyes Adobe Historical Site, you can learn about the widow (Maria Antonia Machado) who purchased the original Rancho Las Virgenes. The Wallis Annenberg Wildlife Crossing, a vegetated overpass spanning the Ventura Freeway and Agoura Road, is designed to allow safe passage for wildlife. It's expected to be completed in 2025.

Visit!

REYES ADOBE HISTORICAL SITE
30400 Rainbow Crest Dr.
818-597-7366

But Laurel Canyon also has a dark history. Three members and an associate of the Wonderland Gang (a group of drug dealers living on Wonderland Avenue) were murdered on July 1, 1981.

Today, the canyon neighborhood has multi-million-dollar homes along most of the canyon road up to Mulholland Drive.

TIP

To see Jim Morrison's former residence (The Love Street House), walk a few feet behind Canyon Country Market to 8021 Rothdell.

Eat!

CANYON COUNTRY STORE
(deli inside)
2108 Laurel Canyon Blvd.
323-654-8091

to Do!

THE LOVE STREET HOUSE
8021 Rothdell

Jim Morrison's former residence

START YOUR DRIVE ON LAUREL CANYON BOULEVARD IN WEST HOLLYWOOD at the Canyon Country Store (a red-brick building on the right corner). Continue driving along Laurel Canyon. Midway, Mulholland Drive intersects on the left. If you stay on Laurel Canyon, you'll reach Studio City and Ventura Boulevard, where you can turn left to continue your next road trip.

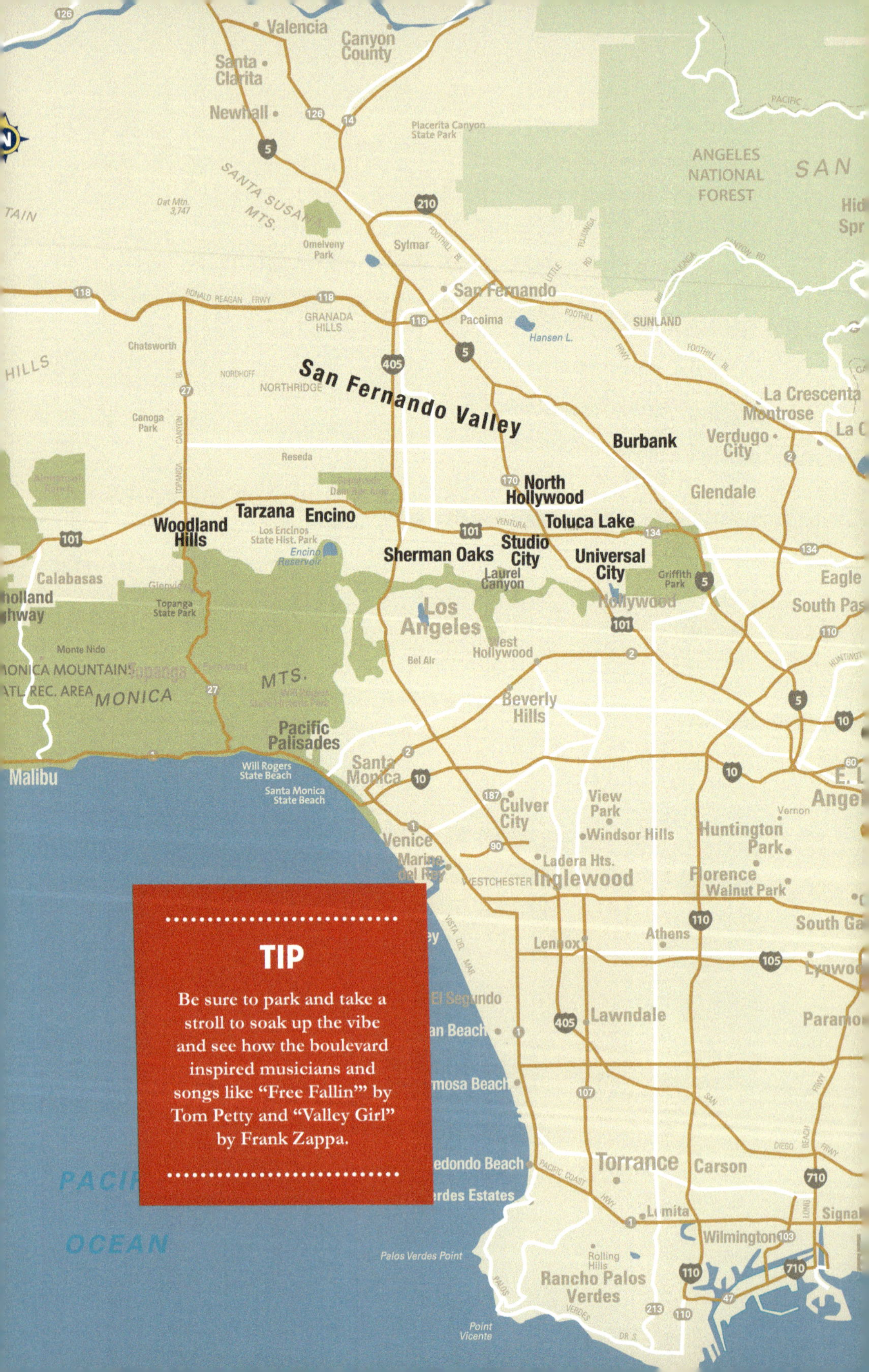

TIP

Be sure to park and take a stroll to soak up the vibe and see how the boulevard inspired musicians and songs like "Free Fallin'" by Tom Petty and "Valley Girl" by Frank Zappa.

VENTURA BOULEVARD/ SAN FERNANDO VALLEY

One of the oldest routes in the San Fernando Valley, Ventura Boulevard follows a portion of the commemorative El Camino Real, which connected California's 21 missions and was used by settlers, missionaries, and travelers. It was also called US Route 101 before the nearby 101 Ventura Freeway was built.

Ventura Boulevard is still a well-traveled route, spanning 18 miles through the communities of Studio City, Sherman Oaks, Encino, Tarzana, and Woodland Hills before reaching the end at Valley Circle Boulevard.

Up and down the boulevard are restaurants, bars, gastropubs, boutiques, stores, and banks. It's where locals, from teens to businesspeople, meet for a meal, chat over coffee, and shop for unique items.

It was during the 1920s and 1930s that Ventura Boulevard experienced substantial growth, attracting the entertainment industry. In 1928, Mack Sennett established Keystone Studios, which produced silent movies. After talkies made their debut, Keystone became Republic Pictures and then CBS Studio Center in 1963.

For more information about Ventura Boulevard and the San Fernando Valley, visit the San Fernando Valley Historical Society at sfvhs.com or call 818-365-7810.

START THIS TOUR AT

THE EASTERN EDGE of Lankershim and Ventura boulevards, head west. Metered street parking is available along the boulevard.

UNIVERSAL CITY

Located a stone's throw from Ventura Boulevard and Studio City, Universal City was developed specifically for the entertainment industry.

Universal Pictures's founder, Carl Laemmle, moved his film studio from New York to Los Angeles in 1912. Three years later, he purchased 230 acres in the San Fernando Valley and created Universal City as a self-contained movie-making community on a former chicken farm.

He began offering tours of his film studio for 25 cents (plus an extra five cents for a boxed chicken lunch). In 1964, the studio opened as a theme park—Universal Studios Hollywood—with rides and a behind-the-scenes studio tour.

Universal Pictures makes up most (about 70 percent) of Universal City, an unincorporated LA neighborhood near the City of Burbank. Universal City; Universal Studios Lot; Universal Studios Hollywood; and Universal CityWalk, a shopping and entertainment center that opened in 1993, lie within Universal City.

The remaining area that lies within LA city limits includes the 10 Universal City Plaza office building, the Sheraton Universal, and Universal Hilton. Both hotels are a good home base for visiting Universal Studios Hollywood.

Stay!

UNIVERSAL CITYWALK
100 Universal City Plaza
800-864-8377

to Do!

UNIVERSAL STUDIOS HOLLYWOOD
100 Universal City Plaza
800-864-8377

Campo de Cahuenga Memorial Park marks the birthplace of California.

STUDIO CITY

Well before Studio City was associated with movie studios—earning its name in the 1920s—it was the site where the Treaty of Cahuenga was signed on January 13, 1847, to end the Mexican–American War.

According to historical records, the treaty was signed by General Andres Pico and Lieutenant Colonel John C. Frémont on the porch of an 1845 adobe house (although archaeologists discovered the house was likely built around 1790). And though the original ranch house was demolished, a replica was rebuilt and dedicated in 1951 as the Campo de Cahuenga Memorial Park, marking the birthplace of California. Campo de Cahuenga is open to the public and contains a small museum with exhibits. It also hosts numerous events with speakers.

The historic Campo is a quiet place ideal for reflecting on the Tongva People, missionaries, and pioneers who walked through here. It was also a stop for the Butterfield Overland Mail stagecoach line. The Campo is listed on the National Register of Historic Places.

TIP

Notice the art mural on a Chase Bank at 12224 Ventura Boulevard, and see the *Brady Bunch* Modernist house, on Dilling Street in North Hollywood. It was used for the sitcom's exterior shots.

The Little Brown Church was founded by Reverend John H. Wells in 1939.

It wasn't until the Los Angeles Aqueduct brought water to the San Fernando Valley in 1913 that Studio City developed as a community. Mack Sennett (a producer, director, and actor) partnered with publisher and investor Harry Chandler to build movie studios and a community for the entertainment industry. Mack Sennett Studio later became the Republic Picture Studio, then CBS Studios/Radford Studios.

Studio City is also home to the famous Little Brown Church, where Ronald Reagan married Nancy Davis on March 4, 1952. Many other celebrities have also exchanged vows in the tiny church, which opened its doors in 1939.

But not all of Studio City's residents are in the entertainment industry. Many simply enjoy the community's proximity to Hollywood, Downtown LA, and the Santa Monica Mountains.

Eat!

ART'S DELICATESSEN
12224 Ventura Blvd.
818-762-1221

CARNEY'S RESTAURANT
12601 Ventura Blvd.
818-761-8300

MICELI'S
3655 Cahuenga Blvd.
323-851-3344

Visit!

LITTLE BROWN CHURCH
4418 Coldwater Canyon Ave.
818-786-4070

Stay!

EL ROYALE HOTEL
11117 Ventura Blvd.
323-829-1860

to Do!

CAMPO DE CAHUENGA PARK
3919 Lankershim Blvd.
818-623-4166
campodecahuenga.com

SHERMAN OAKS

Sherman Oaks is a quiet community that's almost a city unto itself. It's primarily an affluent area, with most of the homes located in the hills.

The Sherman Oaks neighborhood was among the first communities in the San Fernando Valley to develop quickly in the early 20th century. The town is named after General Moses Hazeltine Sherman, who was a partner in the Los Angeles Suburban Homes Co. when he purchased 1,000 acres for himself from a parcel of 47,500 acres and developed the area in 1927. Sherman Way, a street that runs from West Hills to Burbank, is named after him, and Hazeltine Avenue is named after his daughter.

There's an active homeowners' association and a business improvement district. Around 2000, active community members got together to implement a four-year tree-planting project to beautify three miles of Ventura Boulevard.

The heart of Sherman Oaks is the area around Ventura and Van Nuys boulevards, known as the Village at Sherman Oaks Business Improvement District. The boundaries were established in 1999 and encompass a collection of restaurants, boutiques, specialty shops, professional services, and fitness studios. The variety of shops includes an old-school record shop (Freakbeat, selling used and new records and CDs since 2003) and Books on the Boulevard (a used bookstore).

Eat!

CASA VEGA
13301 Ventura Blvd.
818-788-4868

MISTRAL
(French bistro)
13422 Ventura Blvd.
818-981-6650

THE GREAT GREEK
13362 Ventura Blvd.

VALLEY INN RESTAURANT AND MARTINI BAR
4557 Sherman Oaks Ave.
818-784-1163

Visit!

BOOKS ON THE BOULEVARD
13551 Ventura Blvd.
818-905-0988

FREAKBEAT RECORDS
13616 Ventura Blvd.
818-995-7603

TIP

See a collection of local historical artifacts at Valley Relics Museum, 7900 Balboa Boulevard, Van Nuys (entrance on Stagg Street). 818-616-4083

ENCINO

For thousands of years, the area's natural springs were an important water source for Indigenous people, and later for the settlers cultivating the agricultural land with ranches and farms in the late 19th and early 20th centuries.

It wasn't until the mid-20th century that Encino developed into a suburban community. Following WWII, the large ranches were subdivided into residential neighborhoods.

Encino's most prominent historic landmark is the Rancho Los Encinos Adobe, built in 1849. The property was located along a significant road between Santa Barbara and Los Angeles.

TIP

Self-guided tours and docent-led tours are available at the Rancho Los Encinos adobe.

Constructed in 1874 by ranch owner Eugene Garnier, the pond is fed by a natural spring.

The De La Osa Adobe contains exhibits related to the Rancho's various owners over the years.

It's been preserved as a state historic park that includes the original eight-room De La Osa Adobe, the two-story Garnier building, a blacksmith shop, and a natural spring that feeds a pond. The pond was built in 1874 by rancher Eugene Garnier.

Visit!

LOS ENCINOS STATE HISTORIC PARK
16756 Moorpark St.
818-784-4849

TARZANA

Understandably, Tarzana residents are proud that their town is named after Edgar Rice Burroughs's fictional jungle character, Tarzan. Burroughs moved to the area in 1919 from Illinois and purchased the 550-acre estate (called Miraflores) from *Los Angeles Times* publisher General Harrison Gray Otis.

The publisher built a house on his San Fernando Valley property in the late 1800s. There was just a one-lane dirt road leading from Ventura Boulevard to Otis's cabin. The road is still there and is called Otis Drive.

Otis's cabin was the only building in the area until Burroughs built his own house nearby. By 1923, the city of Los Angeles was encroaching, so Burroughs sold much of his land for development. In 1928, the town was incorporated.

TIP

Visit the Tarzana Community & Cultural Center, which features a wall of Tarzan photos. Farther down the street, you can stop by Edgar Rice Burroughs's former office and burial site. His ashes are buried beneath a large walnut tree.

Jon Tsuchiyama, owner of West Valley Nursery, helps tend the garden at the Tarzana Community & Cultural Center.

About two years later, a post office was established, and the 300 residents held a contest to find a name for the new community. The winning entry was Tarzana.

The construction of the Ventura Freeway in the 1950s brought residential and commercial growth to Tarzana—but angst to Shigeru Tsuchiyama, who established West Valley Nursery in 1951. Not only did the freeway cut through his property, but he also worried that people wouldn't drive along Ventura Boulevard anymore. But that didn't happen. The thriving nursery, owned by his son Jon, sits in the same location on busy Ventura Boulevard.

Across the street, the Tarzana Community & Cultural Center is housed in a mid-1940s house on the corner of Vanalden Avenue and Ventura Boulevard. The center is a non-profit organization that preserves Tarzana's history, and serves as a community venue for support groups, classes, and events.

Visit!

CORBIN BOWL (1959)
19616 Ventura Blvd.
818-996-2695

EDGAR RICE BURROUGHS GRAVE SITE
18354 Ventura Blvd.

TARZANA COMMUNITY & CULTURAL CENTER
Garden hours: Monday to Thursday, noon to 5 p.m., and by appointment.
19130 Ventura Blvd.
818-705-1286

WEST VALLEY NURSERY
19035 Ventura Blvd.
818-342-2623

WOODLAND HILLS

When land developer Victor Girard first saw the agricultural fields in the southwestern San Fernando Valley, in the early 1900s, he envisioned a town with small country estates. Critics warned him it was too far from LA. But Girard banked on his success with his first subdivision in LA in 1907.

In 1922, he organized the Boulevard Land Company and purchased 2,886 acres; carved out lots; and planted pepper, sycamore, and eucalyptus trees. He named the new town Girard, officially established in 1923. (The town was renamed Woodland Hills in 1941.) As the town grew, Girard started his own newspaper, *Girard News*, and built stables for his Girard Pick and Spur Club, as well as a golf course for Girard Country Club. He partnered with developers to build a scenic highway (later named Mulholland Highway) through the Santa Monica Mountains. To pay for these improvements, Girard and the Boulevard Land Company borrowed money and added a lien on every property in town—something the homeowners didn't know at the time. Soon, his company was in debt and folded.

Meanwhile, Woodland Hills was attracting Hollywood figures seeking space and privacy. The Motion Picture & Television Fund, a retirement campus for entertainment industry veterans and their spouses, was established in 1921. (The hospital's long-term care unit was dedicated as Mary Pickford House in 2019.)

Van Dekker House

In the 1930s, movie mogul Jack Warner built Warner Ranch, and Mae West bought a home (later replaced by apartments) on Ventura Boulevard. Architect Rudolph Schindler built a house for Albert Van Dekker in 1940.

After WWII, Woodland Hills experienced rapid residential and commercial growth.

Los Angeles Pierce College was founded in 1947 as an agricultural college. Portions of Warner Ranch were sold for the development of businesses, including the Warner Center business district. In 2024, the Los Angeles Rams practice field debuted at West Oxnard Street and Canoga Avenue.

Eat!

ADAGIO RISTORANTE
22841 Ventura Blvd.
818-225-0533

CASALENA
22160 Ventura Blvd.
818-704-1185

MONTY'S
(steaks and seafood)
5371 Topanga Canyon Blvd.
818-716-9736

SAN FERNANDO VALLEY DESTINATIONS

Burbank, Toluca Lake, and North Hollywood are a short drive to Hollywood and Ventura Boulevard.

BURBANK

Burbank is unique in that it's home to major studios, including the Walt Disney Studios, NBC, and Warner Bros., as well as production studios, and yet retains a small-town feel with mom-and-pop businesses. Most of these are in the Magnolia Park district—one of several neighborhoods that include Downtown, the Media District, Equestrian District, and Burbank Hills.

The 1887 Mentzer house is part of the Gordon R. Howard Museum complex.

Burbank is named after its founder, Dr. David Burbank, a dentist from Maine who moved to Los Angeles in 1866. He bought land and built a sheep ranch on what is now the backlot of Warner Bros. Studios.

In 1886 Burbank sold his land for $250,000 to the Providencia Land, Water, and Development Company. The company named the new town Burbank,

Each year Burbank enters a float in the Pasadena Tournament of Roses Parade.

then a small village with farms growing fruit, vegetables, and alfalfa.

As the town grew, Burbank incorporated in 1911. But significant growth began when airplane manufacturer Lockheed moved to Burbank in 1928 (it left in 1990). During WWII, Lockheed employed thousands of men and women, doubling Burbank's population to about 34,000 in the 1940s.

To protect Lockheed from enemy attack, Walt Disney Studios, which had moved to Burbank in 1938, helped camouflage the plant by canvassing the facility to resemble a suburban development from the air.

TIP

Bob's Big Boy hosts a Classic Car Show every Friday, 4-10 p.m.

At Warner Bros. Studio, take a behind-the-scenes tour in an open tram, where you'll see film sets and props and hear about the studio's history.

In 1930, Burbank acquired a small airport, which changed names over the decades until settling on the Hollywood Burbank Airport.

This Bob's Big Boy was built in 1949. It's the oldest remaining Bob's Big Boy in the US.

And yet, Burbank still feels like a quaint hometown, where residents gather for concerts in the hillside Starlight Bowl amphitheater (built in 1951) or meet for a meal at their favorite restaurant.

Over the years, downtown has transformed from the outdoor pedestrian Golden Mall (remember "Beautiful Downtown Burbank," made famous by *Rowan and Martin's Laugh-In* TV show?) to a trendy area with restaurants and theaters.

Eat!

BOB'S BIG BOY
4211 Riverside Dr.
818-843-9334

CHILI JOHN'S (1946)
2018 W Burbank Blvd.
818-846-3611

DON CUCO
218 E Orange Ave.
818-955-8895

GIAMELA'S SUBMARINE SANDWICHES
216 Magnolia Blvd.
818-845-6611

HANDY MARKET
(Saturday outdoor barbecues)
2514 Magnolia Blvd. #22
818-848-2500

LA BAMBA
(casual island cuisine)
2600 N Glenoaks Blvd.
818-846-3358

GRANADA RESTAURANT
1100 W Victory Blvd.
818-843-0313

MONTE CARLO ITALIAN DELI
3103 W Magnolia Blvd.
818-845-3516

SANTORO'S SUBMARINE SANDWICHES
1423 W Burbank Blvd.
818-848-8888

TALLYRAND (1959)
1700 W Olive Ave.
818-846-9904

THE CASTAWAY
(hilltop restaurant with views)
1250 E Harvard Rd.
818-848-6691

THE RAMP RESTAURANT & BAR
7730 N Hollywood Way
818-768-6499

THE SMOKE HOUSE (1949)
4420 Lakeside Dr.
818-845-3731

Visit!

GORDON R. HOWARD MUSEUM
115 N Lomita St.
818-841-6333

STOUGH CANYON PARK
1335 Lockheed View Dr.
818-238-5300

WILDWOOD CANYON PARK
(hiking trails, picnic tables)
1701 Wildwood Canyon Rd.
818-238-5300

Stay!

COAST ANABELLE HOTEL
Boutique hotel with an on-site restaurant and free shuttle service to/from Burbank Airport and area attractions.
2011 W Olive Ave.
818-845-7800

HOTEL AMARANO BURBANK-HOLLYWOOD
(complimentary bicycle rentals)
322 N Pass Ave.
818-842-8887

THE TANGERINE
(built in 1960 as the Holiday Lodge; free breakfast)
3901 W Riverside Dr.
818-843-1121

to Do!

DEBELL GOLF CLUB AND HILLTOP RESTAURANT & BAR
1500 E Walnut Ave.
818-845-0022

LA KINGS ICE AT PICKWICK GARDENS
1001 W Riverside Dr.
818-333-8000

LOS ANGELES EQUESTRIAN CENTER
480 Riverside Dr.
818-840-9063

STARLIGHT BOWL
1249 Lockheed View Dr.
818-238-5397

STOUGH CANYON NATURE CENTER
Exhibits about wildlife, flora, and fauna.
2300 E Walnut Ave.
818-238-5440

WARNER BROS. STUDIO TOUR
3400 Warner Blvd.
818-977-8687

TOLUCA LAKE

Overlapping a small section in the City of Burbank, Toluca Lake is bordered by Universal City, Studio City, and North Hollywood. Situated in an unincorporated part of Los Angeles, Toluca Lake was developed in 1923, and it became a magnet for Hollywood's elite after Warner Bros. opened its studio in 1928.

The community has been home to many celebrities, including Bing Crosby, Bob Hope, and Frankie Avalon. It's also where Ronald and Nancy Reagan held their wedding reception.

The manmade lake (about 10 feet deep) began as a natural spring-fed swampy pond and developed into a six-acre lake for the planned community. The first home built on the lakeshore later became Amelia Earhart's residence.

The lake itself, fed by the Los Angeles River, is surrounded by upscale homes with private docks and is not visible or accessible to the public.

However, Toluca Lake is a warm and welcoming community where you can walk to stores, restaurants, and other businesses.

Eat!

DON CUCO
(Mexican restaurant since 1969)
3911 W Riverside Dr.
818-842-1123

The 1926 El Portal Theatre was built as a vaudeville and silent movie house before the debut of "talkies" in the 1930s.

NORTH HOLLYWOOD (NOHO)

North Hollywood is a district in the San Fernando Valley. In its early days, around 1873, it was a farming village developed by Isaac B. Lankershim and Isaac Newton Van Nuys. Lankershim's son, James B. Lankershim, later created the Lankershim Ranch Land and Water Company and established a town called Toluca in 1887.

The company sold small farms, and the Southern Pacific Railroad established a rail line and station near the present-day North Hollywood Red Line station at Lankershim and Chandler boulevards. The town was renamed Lankershim in 1896.

The completion of the Los Angeles Aqueduct in 1913 fueled the housing boom of the 1910s and 1920s, and several Valley communities agreed to be annexed to the City of LA.

In 1927, the neighborhood was once again renamed, this time to North Hollywood to capitalize on the Hollywood name. The growth of suburbs during WWII and the completion of the 170 Hollywood Freeway transformed North Hollywood from an agricultural to a suburban residential area of LA.

North Hollywood experienced a renaissance with the development of the NoHo Arts District in 1992. It's home to the 1926 restored El Portal Theatre, the Television Academy, art galleries, and several acting and dance studios. NoHo Commons, a mixed-use complex with apartments and eateries, has brought more young people to the area.

NoHo's boundaries are Chandler Boulevard to the north, Cahuenga Boulevard to the east, Tujunga Avenue to the west, and Camarillo Street to the south.

Established in 1941, Idle Hour is an example of programmatic architecture, designed to attract passing motorists.

NoHo Lofts Commons

Eat!

GROUNDWORK COFFEE (1896)
In the historic Lankershim Train Depot
11275 Chandler Blvd.
818-423-2626

IDLE HOUR
The 1933 Group bought and restored the whiskey-barrel-shaped bar that was built in 1941.
4824 Vineland Ave.
323-831-0256

PITFIRE PIZZA
5203 Lankershim Blvd.
818-980-2949

TONGA HUT (1958)
(tiki bar; outside food allowed)
12808 Victory Blvd.
818-769-0708

Visit!

CLASSIC TOYS
12212 Ventura Blvd.
818-980-0032

EL PORTAL THEATRE
(performing arts venue)
5269 Lankershim Blvd.
818-508-0281

TELEVISION ACADEMY
5220 Lankershim Blvd.
818-754-2800

Stay!

THE GARLAND
(and the Front Yard restaurant)
4222 Vineland Ave.
818-980-8000

BAKERSFIELD
JOHAN
58
99
TEHACHAPI
ICOPA
MOJAVE
BORON
FRAIZER PARK
ROSAMOND
39
138
LANCASTER
14
PALMDALE
5
Canyon
County
Acton
138
Saugus
Agua
Dulce
Santa
Clarita
LAKE
CASITAS
Valencia
Newhall
ANGELES
NATIONAL
FOREST
VENTURA
210
OXNARD
LOS
ANGELES
BURBANK
1
PASADENA
HOLLYWOOD
10
BEVERLY
HILLS
SANTA
MONICA
405
710
WHITTIER
CHINO
TORRANCE
ANAHEIM
91
SANTA
ANA
LONG
BEACH
1
5
LAGUNA
BEACH
SANTA
CATALINA
ISLAND
SAN CLEMENTE
OCEANS

SIERRA HIGHWAY

Until the Antelope Valley Freeway (State Highway 14) opened in 1963, Sierra Highway was the main roadway between Santa Clarita and Los Angeles. It's still a much-utilized highway that runs parallel to State Highway 14 and serves as one of the main streets for Palmdale and Lancaster in the Antelope Valley 40 miles away.

Sierra Highway (which follows a portion of historic US Route 6) begins at San Fernando Road and the Old Road near the Golden State (5) and Antelope Valley (14) freeways in Newhall. After Acton, a fork in the road offers options to veer left and stay on Sierra Highway or continue straight onto Pearblossom Highway, which travels through the desert to Wrightwood.

Sierra Highway is flanked by residential neighborhoods, strip malls, and restaurants before becoming rural, with ranches and occasional upscale businesses such as a French restaurant and a winery.

Before Sierra Highway, the main passageway was Beale's Cut, a stagecoach pass built in 1859 near the present-day 5 and 14 freeways. In 1861, landowner Edward Beale extended it. It was the main road through Newhall Pass until the Newhall Auto Tunnel in 1910. The auto tunnel was later replaced by a four-lane road known as Highway 6, then Highway 14, and eventually Sierra Highway.

Many films and TV shows have been filmed along the highway, including the 1936 movie *Modern Times* starring Charlie Chaplin and Paulette Goddard.

In 1971, Steven Spielberg made his first feature-length film *Duel* along Sierra Highway in Canyon Country, Agua Dulce, and Acton.

Le Chene French restaurant, opened in 1980 by chef/owner Juan Alonso, replaced an old gas station from 1915.

START THIS TOUR AT

THE JUNCTION OF THE 5 AND 14 FREEWAYS ON SIERRA HIGHWAY IN NEWHALL.

SIERRA HIGHWAY TRAVELS THROUGH THE SANTA CLARITA TOWNS of Newhall, Canyon Country, Agua Dulce, and Acton. At a fork, Sierra Highway meets Pearblossom Highway. You can stay on Pearblossom to reach Little Rock and Wrightwood or veer left to stay on Sierra Highway through Palmdale and Lancaster.

SANTA CLARITA

Steeped in Western history and the location for many films and TV shows, Santa Clarita is in the Santa Clarita Valley, about 30 miles northwest of downtown LA. The area's mountains and valleys provided the perfect backdrop for Western films starting around 1900. Western actors William S. Hart and Harry Carey had ranches in the area.

The valley's history dates even further to the 1800s, when Phineas Banning (the same man who developed Wilmington) carved out Newhall Pass in 1854. Today, the Golden State Freeway travels through the Newhall Pass, connecting Santa Clarita to the San Fernando Valley and Los Angeles.

Santa Clarita was primarily developed by American businessman Henry Mayo Newhall, who purchased land and established the towns of Newhall and Saugus in 1875. His five sons incorporated the Newhall Land and Farming Company in 1883 and further developed the area, which incorporated as the City of Santa Clarita in 1987. It encompasses the communities of Newhall, Saugus, Canyon Country, and Valencia.

The roadside Halfway House Cafe, which started as a trading post in 1906, has been serving hearty breakfast and lunch items since 1931. The old-timey appearance makes it a favorite location spot with the entertainment industry.

Communities within the valley but not part of the City of Santa Clarita include Agua Dulce, Castaic, and Stevenson Ranch (this development lies within LA city jurisdiction).

Santa Clarita's natural spaces, numerous hiking trails, parks, history, award-winning public schools, and proximity to LA attract many families.

The area is home to three colleges (including the California Institute of the Arts), two Six Flags theme parks, and the company headquarters for Princess Cruises.

Eat!

ANNA'S ARMENIAN BAKERY
16507 Soledad Canyon Rd.
661-367-6305

BROTHER'S BURGERS
20655 Soledad Canyon Rd.
661-299-9278

HALFWAY HOUSE CAFÉ (1931)
15564 Sierra Hwy.
661-251-0102

LA COCINA
(family-owned Mexican restaurant and bar)
28022 Seco Canyon Rd.
661-297-4546

28076 Bouquet Canyon Rd.
661-513-0142

19915 Golden Valley Rd.
661-250-7141

Visit!

THE GENTLE BARN
15825 Sierra Hwy.
661-252-2440

NEWHALL

Named after businessman Henry Mayo Newhall, Newhall is the oldest neighborhood in the City of Santa Clarita and embraces its Western heritage in Old Town Newhall.

Much of Santa Clarita's history begins in Newhall, with California's first gold discovery by rancher Francisco Lopez in 1842. But it was the discovery of oil in the Santa Susana mountains that put Newhall on the map. Charles Mentry operated the first successful oil well, Pico No. 4, and created the town of Mentryville. The oil-drilling boomtown thrived with families and workers from 1876 to 1900. Today, Mentryville is a ghost town with several standing structures and hiking trails.

Western actor William S. Hart played a big role in putting a spotlight on Newhall. The 1920s silent film star built a 22-room hilltop mansion and ranch there. He bequeathed his property to the County of LA to be used as a public park and museum. It's a popular park with several historic structures, hiking trails, and picnic areas. As of December 2024, plans were underway to transfer ownership of Hart Park from the City of LA to the City of Santa Clarita by the summer of 2025.

Old Town Newhall is a lively place with restaurants, shops, and events.

The Hart Ranch House contains William S. Hart's personal belongings, cowboy memorabilia, and Western art.

The area's historic district is Old Town Newhall, which encompasses shops, restaurants, theaters, a library, and the Western Walk of Stars (featuring plaques of Western stars' names). There's also a weekly farmers market, various events, and live shows at Canyon Theater. Located adjacent to Old Town Newhall Library is Old Newhall Jail, a historical landmark. Completed in 1906, it served as a jail and constable's office until 1926, when a sheriff's substation opened; the jail was used until 1939. Since then, various businesses have occupied the space. The building was purchased by Manny Santana in 1989.

TIP

Take a morning hike in Hart Park. A one-quarter-mile nature trail leads to Hart's mansion. The one-mile Bison Road passes enclosed bison, descendants of a herd donated by Walt Disney in 1962.
661-259-1750

Visit!

MENTRYVILLE PARK
27201 Pico Canyon Rd.
323-221-9944

OLD NEWHALL JAIL
24522 Spruce St.

SANTA CLARITA HISTORY CENTER
24107 Newhall Ave.
661-254-1275

to Do!

EAST AND RICE CANYON
(hiking trails with a seasonal stream)
24255 The Old Rd.

TOWSLEY CANYON PARK
(hiking and seasonal stream)
24335 The Old Rd.
661-255-2937

WILLIAM S. HART PARK AND MUSEUM
24151 Newhall Ave.
661-254-4584

BREWERY DRACONUM
(restaurant)
24407 Main St.
661-568-9160

BRICKS
23820 Lyons Ave.
661-286-1091

DAILY HARVEST CAFÉ
22722 Lyons Ave.
661-888-8620

EAT REAL ON MAIN
24450 Main St.
661-753-3450

EGG PLANTATION
24415 Walnut St.
661-255-8222

EIGHTH & RAIL
22505 8th St.
661-255-7833

LILY'S CAFÉ
23700 Lyons Ave.
661-259-9656

NEWHALL PRESS ROOM
24257 Main St.
661-753-3454

NEWHALL REFINERY
24258 Main St.
661-388-4477

OLD TOWN JUNCTION
24275 Main St.
661-702-4888

POCOCK BREWING PUBLIC HOUSE
24329 Main St.
661-578-5990

ROSE AND CROWN BRITISH RESTAURANT
24246 Lyons Ave.
661-255-5048

THE LOAF JAPANESE BAKERY & CAFÉ
24450 Main St. #160
661-476-5194

WAY STATION COFFEE SHOP
(breakfast and lunch)
24377 Main St.
661-255-0222

Stay!

LEXEN NEWHALL
24219 Railroad Ave.
661-505-7500

DRIVE ALONG SIERRA HIGHWAY.

CANYON COUNTRY

Located in the central and eastern parts of the City of Santa Clarita, Canyon Country is a residential and commercial neighborhood in the Soledad and Mint Canyon areas. It was named Canyon Country in 1968.

Area history dates to the mid-1800s, when Colonel Thomas Mitchell created the area's first school, Sulphur Springs Elementary.

Within Santa Clarita, which covers about 52 square miles, Canyon Country is one of the largest communities. It's home to about 93,000 residents.

The family-owned Backwoods Inn has been on Sierra Highway since 1966.

Eat!

BACKWOODS INN
17846 Sierra Hwy.
661-252-5522

CHI-CHI'S PIZZA
27117 Sierra Hwy.
661-252-4405

CONTINUE ON SIERRA HIGHWAY.

AGUA DULCE

Home to about 3,500 residents, this rural community has equestrian properties and scenic landscapes. The most famous is Vasquez Rocks Natural Area, a unique rock formation that got its name from the bandit Tiburcio Vasquez, who hid in the rocks.

Vasquez Rocks has been a popular film location for numerous movies, including *The Flintstones, Blazing Saddles*, and the film *Duel*. Many music videos have also been shot here.

But Vasquez Rocks is also popular with those who enjoy hiking and exploring natural wonders.

In addition, the Pacific Crest Trail, which runs from Mexico to Canada, travels through Agua Dulce.

Eat!

LE CHENE
12625 Sierra Hwy.
661-251-4315

Visit!

AGUA DULCE WINERY
9640 Sierra Hwy.
661-268-7402

VAZQUEZ ROCKS NATURAL AREA
10700 Escondido Canyon Rd.
661-268-0840

Stay!

SIERRA PELONA MOTEL
12117 Sierra Hwy.
661-252-1700

to Do!

Join a **VAZQUEZ ROCKS TWILIGHT HIKE**. Free, but registration required.
10700 Escondido Canyon Rd.
661-268-0840

Agua Dulce Winery vineyard

FROM AGUA DULCE, stay on Sierra Highway to Acton.

'49ER SALOON (1870)
31908 Crown Valley Rd.
661-526-4414

LA CABANA RESTAURANT
2370 Soledad Canyon Rd.
661-269-4504

ACTON

Acton is a small, rural town home to about 7,300 people.

Situated near the Antelope Valley, it's known for its equestrian-friendly atmosphere and has a mix of residential and rural properties.

It was a railroad camp from 1873 to 1876 during the construction of the Southern Pacific Railroad in the Saugus–Mojave section. The Acton Depot opened in October 1876.

Acton was founded in 1887 by gold miners and was named after Acton, Massachusetts. The mining of gold, copper, and titanium in the Red Rover Mine and the Governor Mine continued into the early 1900s. The Governor Mine was named after then-governor Henry T. Gage, who advocated to relocate the state capital from Sacramento to Acton.

John F. Duehren, Acton's first resident, opened a saloon to provide refreshments to the miners and prospectors in 1870—and it's still operating. His son-in-law, Richard E. Nickels, is credited with developing the frontier town and amenities in 1887. He also opened Acton's first hotel in 1889, and published the area's first newspaper, the *Acton Rooster*, starting in 1891.

TWO OPTIONS: Sierra Highway meets Pearblossom Highway, which leads to the small desert towns of Little Rock and Pearblossom.

OR, VEER LEFT at the fork to stay on Sierra Highway to Palmdale and Lancaster.

PALMDALE

Palmdale is a desert town about 60 miles from LA. It was the first city in the Antelope Valley to incorporate, in 1962.

Although it's quite the commute on a workday, people move here for affordable housing. But Palmdale's remote location also accommodates the aerospace industry.

The area was settled in the 1800s, spurred by the gold rush, cattle ranching, and the completion of the Southern Pacific Railroad in 1876.

The town was originally called Palmenthal (German for "palm valley") by early homesteaders who were mostly German, French, and Midwestern farmers.

The completion of the California aqueduct in 1913 brought more growth. Palmdale's aerospace history began in 1933 when the US government built Edwards Air Force Base (originally called Muroc).

In 1952, the Palmdale Airport and US Air Force Plant 42 opened, bringing in Lockheed Martin, Boeing, and Northrop Grumman. Palmdale became a giant employer in the aerospace industry.

Palmdale has two excellent aerospace attractions open to the public. The outdoor Blackbird Airpark is located on Plant 42 property, an annex of the Air Force Flight Test Museum at Edwards Air Force Base. It's the only place in the world where you can see Lockheed SR-71 and A-12 aircrafts side by side, as well as more than 80 other specialized aircraft.

The adjacent Joe Davies Heritage Airpark contains a growing collection of vintage aircraft and exhibits. The collection of aircraft was flown, tested, designed, produced, or modified at Plant 42.

NASA aircraft at Joe Davies Heritage Airpark

Visit!

BLACKBIRD AIRPARK
2503 E Ave. P
661-274-0884

JOE DAVIES HERITAGE AIRPARK
2001 E Ave. P
661-267-5611

LITTLEROCK RESERVOIR
Highway 138 and Cheseboro Rd.

DRIVE NORTH on Sierra Highway.

LANCASTER

Lancaster was just a train stop between Bakersfield and Los Angeles until the completion of the Southern Pacific Railroad from San Francisco to Los Angeles in 1876. The railroad's completion signaled the development of Lancaster.

Among the first buildings was the Antelope Valley Hotel, built by the Gilroy family around 1888. It was renamed the Gillwyn Hotel until it was purchased in 1902 by George T. Webber, who operated it as the Western Hotel. It was designated a California Historic Landmark in 1958. It's the oldest surviving building in Lancaster and today serves as a small museum.

By 1890, Lancaster was in the early stages of development. Gold was discovered in the hills north of Lancaster in 1898, attracting prospectors. That same year, borax was found in the mountains, establishing the world's largest borax mine.

Lancaster, which incorporated in 1977, is home to over 172,000 residents of diverse backgrounds.

TIP

Visit the Western Hotel Museum to learn about area history. The museum is open on select days, so be sure to call the Lancaster Museum of Art and History before you go.

661-723-6250

Eat!

LUCKY LUKE PUB
735 W Lancaster Blvd.
661-522-3775

Springtime in Antelope Valley
California Poppy Valley Reserve

The Western Hotel Museum contains photographs and artifacts that depict the town's history

Visit!

ANTELOPE VALLEY INDIAN MUSEUM STATE HISTORIC PARK
15701 E Ave. M
661-946-3055

LANCASTER MUSEUM OF ART AND HISTORY
665 W Lancaster Blvd.
661-723-6250

ANTELOPE VALLEY RURAL MUSEUM
(exhibits with photos, artifacts, and clothes)
2551 W Ave. H
(enter through Gate 3)
661-478-4841

THE BLVD MARKET
(farmers market, Thursdays, 4 p.m. to 9 p.m.)
758 West Lancaster Boulevard and Date Avenue

WESTERN HOTEL MUSEUM
557 W Lancaster Blvd.
661-723-6250

to Do!

LANCASTER PERFORMING ARTS CENTER
750 W Lancaster Blvd.
661-723-5950

ANTELOPE VALLEY CALIFORNIA POPPY RESERVE
Wildflower season is mid-February through May.
15101 Lancaster Rd.
661-724-1180

VALENCIA

Although Six Flags Magic Mountain is located just outside city limits, it's associated with Valencia, a planned community built in the 1960s in phases by the Newhall Land and Farming Company.

The community has miles of paved, landscaped paseos with bridges and tunnels that enable pedestrians and bicyclists to safely navigate the city without crossing streets. The paseo network connects neighborhoods and leads to the Santa Clara River Trail, which travels east along the Santa Clara River to Canyon Country.

The community has golf courses, shopping centers, an industrial area, and numerous restaurants. Six Flags Magic Mountain has been a major attraction since 1971; Six Flags Hurricane Harbor opened in 1995. Princess Cruises moved its headquarters from Century City to Valencia in 2001.

Despite modern attractions, you can still find Western history. Tucked in a residential neighborhood, the Tesoro Adobe was home to silent screen actor Harry Carey, who is credited with helping to establish the Santa Clarita valley as a filming location. In 1916, he built his ranch, which was used

The 1898 railroad trestle bridge and Iron Horse Trailhead in Valencia.

Tesoro Adobe was home to silent screen actor Harry Carey.

> **TIP**
>
> Walk or bike on a paseo. The Iron Horse Trailhead, a four-mile path, was incorporated with the historic 1898 railroad trestle bridge, which connects to the South Fork Trail. The bridge was placed there after the St. Francis Dam disaster in 1928 destroyed the original one.

in many movies and was home to horses, cattle, goats, and other animals.

The Carey family sold the ranch in the mid-1940s, and the Clougherty family (owners of Farmer John) bought the property in 1952. It was donated as Tesoro Adobe Historic Park by the developers (Montalvo Properties, LLC) of the Tesoro community to LA County in 2005.

Visit!

SIX FLAGS HURRICANE HARBOR
(open June to September)
26101 Magic Mountain Pkwy.
661-255-4100

SIX FLAGS MAGIC MOUNTAIN
26101 Magic Mountain Pkwy.
661-255-4100

TESORO ADOBE HISTORIC PARK
29350 Avenida Rancho Tesoro
661-286-4115

Eat!

AZUL TEQUILA MEXICAN GRILL & BAR
25387 Wayne Mills Pl.
661-254-5500

COPPER HILL BBQ
28295 Newhall Ranch Rd.
661-243-3933

ITALIA PANETTERIA & DELI
27674 Newhall Ranch Rd. #55
661-294-9069

NEALIE'S SKILLET
25858 Tournament Rd.
661-678-0031

POCOCK BREWING CO.
24907 Ave. Tibbitts #B
661-775-4899

TEMAKITTO
28126 Newhall Ranch Rd.
661-678-0820

WOLF CREEK RESTAURANT & BREWING CO.
27746 McBean Pkwy.
661-263-9653

SAUGUS

The community of Saugus was initially named Newhall by Henry Mayo Newhall. In 1879, after shifting the town's borders a few miles south, he renamed it Saugus after his birthplace in Saugus, Massachusetts.

Many of the early residents migrated from Texas and Oklahoma to work in the oil fields. But the rural landscape also attracted those seeking space away from the city.

Cowboy movie star Hoot Gibson built a 35-acre ranch and rodeo grounds along the railroad tracks and Soledad Canyon Road in 1924. The rural landscape attracted Hollywood filmmakers, who used his ranch as a movie set.

In 1937, William and Mary Bonelli bought the ranch, where they held rodeos and built a quarter-mile dirt track. Named the Bonelli Ranch Stadium, it was the site for many events featuring midget cars, roadsters, and later stockcars. The track was expanded, and the name changed to Saugus Speedway, which operated as a racetrack from 1939 to 1995.

The grounds have been used for the family-owned Santa Clarita Swap Meet since 1963.

Saugus has other noteworthy historical places. The Original Saugus Cafe, which is the oldest operating restaurant in LA County, opened in 1886 at the north end of the Saugus Train Station. When James Herbert Tolfree opened the diner it was called the Saugus Eating House and was a handy stop for hungry travelers. In 1905, the diner moved across the street to its current location on Railroad Avenue. Throughout its history, many celebrities and dignitaries (including US presidents Benjamin Harrison and Theodore Roosevelt) have dined at the café. It changed ownership a few times and the name eventually became the Original Saugus Café. Under longtime owner Alfredo Mercado, the old-school diner continues to serve comfort food and provide a cozy ambiance.

Visit!

SANTA CLARITA SWAP MEET AT SAUGUS SPEEDWAY
(Tuesdays and Sundays)
22500 Soledad Canyon Rd.
661-259-3886

to Do!

CENTRAL PARK
27150 Bouquet Canyon Rd.
661-290-2240

San Francisquito Creek Trail

Eat!

GYROMANIA GREEK KITCHEN
20655 Soledad Canyon Rd.
661-252-4976

THE ORIGINAL SAUGUS CAFE
25861 Railroad Ave.
661-259-7886

UMAICHI RAMEN
26877 Bouquet Canyon Rd.
661-296-8362

RIDGECREST
395
178
14
JOHANNESBURG
MOJAVE
BORON
ROSAMOND
138
395
LANCASTER
14
PALMDALE
Little Rock
138
Pearblossom
15
5
18
ANGELES
NATIONAL
FOREST
210
BURBANK
38
PASADENA
HOLLYWOOD
BEVERLY
HILLS
10
WHITTIER
CHINO
405
710
RIVERSIDE
TORRANCE
ANAHEIM
91
SANTA
ANA
15
LONG
BEACH
1
5
LAGUNA
BEACH

PEARBLOSSOM HIGHWAY (ROUTE 138)

Soon after turning onto Pearblossom Highway, you'll see twisted Joshua trees, grasses, and other native plants—even tumbleweeds in windy weather—on both sides of this desert highway.

Along the way are eateries, shops, motels, gas stations, dollar stores, and produce stands, as well as boarded-up shops and dirt lots. You'll also pass the California Aqueduct.

Towns here are in the Antelope Valley, a high desert area about 70 miles from the City of Los Angeles. The Antelope Valley is a 3,000-square-mile area that straddles northern Los Angeles County and southern Kern County.

The Antelope Valley was a trade route for Native Americans traveling from Arizona and New Mexico to California's coast.

The communities of Palmdale and Lancaster are located within the valley and are accessible via the 14 Freeway and Sierra Highway.

START THIS TOUR AT

SIERRA HIGHWAY, stay right to merge onto Pearblossom Highway.

LITTLEROCK

Named after the Little Rock Wash that passes through the area, Littlerock is a small town sparsely populated with quaint markets and eateries along Highway 138.

People driving on this route usually stop at Charlie Brown Farms, a sprawling old-timey gift store with aisles stuffed with all sorts of candy, honey, homemade fudge, sodas, toys, Christmas decorations, and other items. The on-site café serves BBQ, sandwiches, salads, breakfast wraps, funnel cakes, and date shakes.

Visit!

CHARLIE BROWN FARMS
8317 Pearblossom Hwy.
661-944-2606

JACKRABBIT FLATS WILDLIFE SANCTUARY
36202 116th St. E
661-944-6881

CRAFTERS VILLAGE & WIND TOYS
8300 Pearblossom Hwy. (across from Charlie Brown Farms)
661-485-7038

Eat!

LITTLEROCK GRILL
7660 Pearblossom Hwy.
661-944-3225

Charlie Brown Farms is a popular roadside stop. in the desert.

PEARBLOSSOM

Pearblossom Highway is the main street through this small desert town, home to nearly 2,500 people. A few small eateries and a market are the primary businesses.

But the town is just a 10-minute drive to the Devil's Punchbowl Natural Area and Nature Center. The 1,310-acre park has unique rock formations, hiking trails, and picnic areas with grills. The nature center has exhibits and photos about area wildlife and plants.

Visit!

DEVIL'S PUNCHBOWL NATURAL AREA AND NATURE CENTER
28000 Devils Punchbowl Rd.
661-944-2743

TOWN & COUNTRY MARKET
13012 Pearblossom Hwy. #3002
661-944-4136

Eat!

GOURMETACOS
12822 Pearblossom Hwy.
661-227-2396

INDEX